STEPS
to the
Altar

Why a Chosen Generation Is Living
Ashamed at the Altar

TOBE MOMAH

WESTBOW®
PRESS
A DIVISION OF THOMAS NELSON
& ZONDERVAN

Foreword by Evangelist Tim Todd.

Scripture taken from the King James Version of the Bible.

WestBow Press books may be ordered through booksellers or by contacting:

WestBow Press
A Division of Thomas Nelson & Zondervan
1663 Liberty Drive
Bloomington, IN 47403
www.westbowpress.com
1 (866) 928-1240

ISBN: 978-1-4908-3085-8 (sc)
ISBN: 978-1-4908-3084-1 (hc)
ISBN: 978-1-4908-3086-5 (e)

Printed in the United States of America.

Library of Congress Control Number: 2014905423

WestBow Press rev. date: 03/26/2014

To a generation of born-again believers called the Acharon generation (Psalm 102:18). They are those the Bible says will be the last generation. They will welcome the King of Kings and the Lord of Lords to earth in His glory. Maranatha, Lord Jesus. May this generation welcome You, our Messiah.

Contents

Foreword

Over the years I've fielded many questions about shame, so I'm always on the lookout for a comprehensive and anointed guide for people dealing with shame. Frankly, I don't have all the answers, but I know that Jesus Christ, through the blood that He poured out, is THE answer.

Thus, it was great for me to find out about S.T.E.P.S. TO THE ALTAR by Dr. Tobe Momah. It is a tremendous source for the important information and instruction that every believer needs and is sometimes embarrassed to ask others about. I believe this book is valuable and important.

You should read this book voraciously and keep it around when you are faced with the pit falls and speed bumps of shame. Dr. Momah espouses a tremendous prescription that captured my complete attention.

Every reader will find much that will contribute to bringing about the complete deliverance you need from the unnecessary bondage of shame.

Dr. Tim Todd
President/Executive Director
Revival Fires International Monroe, Louisiana USA
www.RevivalFires.com

Preface

On my way to Nigeria to celebrate my father's seventieth birthday, God told me to put down in print the words you are about to read. On that jumbo jet, thousands of miles above humanity but in the confines of my Savior, I started writing this book.

God said He wanted a statement about our "would be" golden generation labeled by some as a wasted generation. He revealed to me in a few minutes how we could restore waste places in our generation and make it the glorious generation "without spot or wrinkle" (Ephesians 5:27) that welcomes back the Messiah.

The three and a half months following were busy and bustling with revelation and supernatural insight on the topic of shame. I had never heard a sermon on shame, and the majority of what I put in print was divine thoughts marshaled into human minds for kingdom expression.

My prayer is that this book will transform the dour and meaningless Christian into a glorious vessel used by God to reclaim the earth for His glory. Through this book, I pray the "the earth shall be filled with the knowledge of the glory of the Lord, as the waters cover the sea" (Habakkuk 2:14). Happy reading.

Tobe Momah, MD, FAAFP

Acknowledgments

God inspired this book. He gave the words and allowed me to put them in print. It, however, would not have been possible without other invaluable people along the journey who saw value in it and spurred me on.

More than anyone else, though, my wife of ten years, Rita, provided a setting that encouraged me and sharpened my desire to write. She motivated and mentored me on several of the topics treated here, especially when it concerned females. It would have been almost impossible to finish this book without her invaluable support.

My church, the Assembly West Monroe, Louisiana, and my pastor, Shane Warren, inspired me to keep writing with their heartfelt worship, exceptional warmth and care, and the trailblazing Word. These enabling surroundings helped the dream of this book become a reality. I thank Andy and Janice Varino's Sunday school class, where I shared much of the material in this book, for their rapt attention and bold encouragement.

My parents, Dr. and Mrs. Momah, continue to inspire me with their unconditional love and steadfast loyalty. They have supported my outlandish projects again and again and can be relied upon for untiring camaraderie whenever I need it. My brothers and sisters—Amaka, Ada, Emeka, and Nkem—were all instrumental in this book's completion, and I cannot overemphasize the importance of their help.

Also, thanks to the best publisher in the world, Westbow Press, for its excellent staff and people-management skills. They were invaluable and second to none throughout the project.

I thank the supporter of my ministry, Faith and Power Ministries, for its ardent support and unflinching loyalty. It spurred the publishing of this book with fervent enthusiasm and spirit when I shared portions of it at our monthly Holy Ghost Nights meetings or in correspondence. May what you have made happen in my life be replenished multiple times in yours, in Jesus' name, amen.

Introduction

God created the church for an all-comer's glorious experience and a no-holds-barred, unashamed existence. The STEPS to the altar, meaning shame, tactics, emptiness, powerlessness, and superficiality, as chronicled in the acronym STEPS, explain this paradox. A church birthed in glory cannot be living in shame and expect heaven's approval.

Shame is not an oft-discussed subject in the church. In Jesus' time, this was also the case. In Luke 4, He read from Isaiah and was almost killed by the rampaging mob (Luke 4:28–29) for speaking the truth. That truth includes Isaiah 61:6–7: "In their [the Gentiles'] glory shall ye boast yourselves [and] for your shame ye shall have double."

The antishame and glorious gospel is necessary if Jesus is to return (Ephesians 5:27). A life of shame is a life infinitely paralyzed by insecurity, intimidation, and inferiority. Until the church appropriates the glory given to it by the death and resurrection of Jesus Christ, we cannot eliminate the shame that has unfortunately become the toga of many Christians.

Part I

Shamed or Shamefaced?

Jesus is coming for a glorious church—not a garbage church.

Chapter One

An Epidemic of Shame

And if thou wilt make me an altar of stone, thou shall not build it of hewn stone for if thou lift up thy tool upon it, thou hast polluted (or shamed) it.
—Exodus 20:25

Shame in the Bible has multiple definitions depending on the context. The most common definitions in the Old and New Testaments define shame as a disgrace, a disappointment borne out of delay, or disfigurement, or a loss of face that causes opposition in distribution or intensity.

What has stopped many from finishing strong in life is shame. Their impetus was ebbed and their momentum was curtailed by an incident or accident that was a source of shame in their lives and cost them their destinies.

The body of Christ has stayed oblivious to this serpentine spirit of shame for too long. We have called it victim mentality and labeled them wounded warriors, the battered brigade, or spoiled saints. This is wrong. These Christians are not victims but victors in Christ who need to know they don't have to live with shame another day of their lives.

Unseen Shame

This epidemic of shame is happening in the most evangelical or "saved" nation in the world, the United States. It has the world's largest Christian population (246,780,000), about 80 percent of the population[1] and has been responsible for more global missions work than any other nation in history.

In the words of the 2010 National Intimate Partner and Sexual Violence Survey (NISVS), the United States is experiencing an epidemic of sexual violence.[2] Twenty-four people per minute are victims of rape, sexual violence, or stalking by an intimate partner, and nearly one in five women has been a victim of rape. Of this population, 80 percent are under age twenty-four.

Other sources of unseen shame in the United States include cyberbullying, which involves using technology such as cell phones or the Internet to harm someone. Current estimates are that over half of young people have been bullied online or engaged in it themselves. As many as 20 percent experience cyberbullying regularly, and one in five teens has sent sexually suggestive or nude pictures of himself or herself to others.[3]

Pornography is another source of unseen shame in the US church. Fifty percent of all Christian men and 20 percent of all Christian women in the United States say they are addicted to pornography.[4] An estimated nine out of ten boys and six out of ten girls are exposed to pornography before age eighteen and, as a result, engage in explicit sexual behaviors or sex itself.

Shamefaced—Not Shamed

The Greek word used in 1 Timothy 2:9 for *shamefacedness* is interpreted as modest, holding in awe or reverence, and keeping good perception. It is used for the adornment of a woman in the church and typifies how we, the church, should carry and conduct ourselves.

There is no middle ground; The church lives in shame or in shamefacedness but not both. Jesus said in Luke 4:18 that the Spirit of the Lord was upon Him to preach the gospel and set the captives free so they would receive "for their shame double and for confusion rejoice in their portion" (Isaiah 61:7).

When we as the body of Christ tolerate shame by excusing the inexcusable and allowing the unallowable, we negate the salvation

Jesus died to purchase for us. We are supposed to go from a life of shame to one of glory and not perpetuate shame in our lives.

In 1 Peter 2:9–10, we read, "Ye are a chosen generation, a royal priesthood, an holy nation, a peculiar people that ye should show forth the praises of him who hath called you out of darkness into his marvelous light."

Raped, Robbed, and Restored

I recently counseled a family with a fifteen-year-old daughter who, unbeknownst to them, had been raped several times by her cousin's boyfriend. The incident came to light only because in the review of her laboratory work, I discovered she had a sexually transmitted disease even though she claimed to be a virgin.

On hearing the revelation, she broke down in tears and sobbed continuously for hours. I had to invite the child and family counselor to comfort her. She confided in me and her mom about the repetitive assaults she had endured at the hand of this child predator.

Her life had gone from glory to shame in one moment by an illicit, covert, and traumatic sexual encounter. I encouraged her to look at herself as God sees her, a total treasure, not a heap of garbage as the Enemy would want her to think.

Last time I saw her, she said they were prosecuting the villain, she is excited about school, and most important of all, she has a personal relationship with Jesus Christ and is excited about church again. Her sexual life was raped, her innocence was robbed, but Jesus came to restore it all. Hallelujah!

1. Kosmin B, Keysar A. "American Religious Identification Survey" (ARIS 2008). Trinity college summary report. March 2009.
2. Black, M.C., Basile, K.C., Breiding, M.J., Smith, S.G., Walters, M.L., Merrick, M.T., Chen, J., & Stevens, M.R. (2011). The National Intimate Partner and Sexual Violence Survey (NISVS): 2010 Summary Report. Atlanta, GA: National Center for Injury Prevention and Control, Centers for Disease Control and Prevention.

3. The National Campaign to Prevent Teen and Unplanned Pregnancy, CosmoGirl.com. Sex and Tech: Results From a Survey of Teens Q:10 and Young Adults. Washington, DC; 2008.
4. "Evangelicals are addicted to porn." ChristiaNet – The worldwide Christian community (2006).

You are not a sinner because you sin; You sin because you are a sinner.

Chapter Two

Solution to Shame

Moreover whom he did predestinate, them he also called and whom he called,
them he also justified and whom he justified, them he also glorified.
—Romans 8:30

Shame is an anathema in the kingdom of God. It has a permanent embargo and sanction in God's presence and was summarily eliminated by the death of Jesus on the cross. Isaiah 45:16–17 says,

> They shall be ashamed, and also confounded, all of them:
> they shall go to confusion together that are makers of idols.
> But Israel shall be saved in the LORD with an everlasting
> salvation: ye shall not be ashamed nor confounded world
> without end.

When the prophet Isaiah penned the words of Isaiah 45 thousands of years ago, he did not know how long the world would last, but he knew shame had a termination point when it met with His salvation.

When shame is eliminated, you get double for your troubles. Isaiah 61:6–7 says, "Ye shall be named the Priests of the LORD: men shall call you the Ministers of our God: ye shall eat the riches of the Gentiles, and in their glory shall ye boast yourselves. For your shame ye shall have double."

The message of the cross is incomplete until it removes shame and replaces it with glory. The God of glory declares His "glory shall be revealed, and all flesh shall see it together for the mouth of the Lord hath spoken it" (Isaiah 40:5).

Magnify Christ in Your Body

Paul says in Philippians 1:20 that

> according to his earnest expectation and hope, that in nothing he shall be ashamed, but that with all boldness, as always, so now also Christ shall be magnified in his body, whether it be by life, or by death.

Paul put on Christ and as a result never walked in shame. That is our Christian heritage. It is a choice and is subject to our will. If we submit all to Jesus Christ, we will live life never ashamed again. The Israelites refused God in Jeremiah 13:11 and ended up in shame: "They might be unto me for a people, and for a name, and for a praise, and for a glory but they would not hear." God does not give us shame to partake in but gives us grace and glory. Psalm 84:11 says, "God is a sun and shield [and] the Lord will give grace and glory."

Nothing stops shame like the blood of Jesus. In 1 Corinthians 6:20, we read, "Ye are bought with a price: therefore glorify God in your body, and in your spirit, which are God's." Jesus paid for our glory with His precious blood and gives no room for shame to exist in our now-redeemed glorious life if we accept His finished work on the cross of Calvary.

Who you give yourself to will be exalted in your life. Who you give control to and what influences you most will determine how you end your journey. It can end in shame or celebration depending on your choice.

Glory—Like Father, Like Sons

In John 17:22, Jesus prayed to the Father, "The glory which thou gave me I have given them that they may be one, even as we are one." You are not an orphan but a son of God and a joint heir with Christ of

God's everlasting glory. Romans 8:17 says we are "children [and] then ... heirs of God, and joint-heirs with Christ if so be that we suffer with him, that we may be also glorified together."

Before your birth, God already earmarked you for glory. Romans 8:29–30 says,

> Whom he did foreknow, he also did predestinate to be conformed to the image of his Son, that he might be the firstborn among many brethren. Moreover whom he did predestinate, them he also called: and whom he called, them he also justified: and whom he justified, them he also glorified.

You are the reason for everything Jesus did. He made you "in his image and in his likeness" (Genesis 1:26) and "crowned you with glory and honor" (Psalm 8:5) to have fellowship with Him and be a part of the heavenly family. Just as He is glorious, so must you be glorified.

It is not a father and elder son–only glory enterprise. He wants all sons of God glorified. In Hebrews 2:10, we read, "It became him, for whom are all things, and by whom are all things, in bringing many sons unto glory, to make the captain of their salvation perfect through sufferings."

From Shame to Surplus

I was born the third son of a military professional and an astute teacher. In my teens, I started having weekly debilitating, deleterious asthma attacks. I was ferried to clinics but continued to have asthma exacerbations frequently. On one occasion, I was rushed to the hospital, and my parents had to come and pick me up from high school.

I was entering the house when I heard my father speaking in low tones to my mother. He said, "Tobe is an invalid and should desist from any form of activity."

I behaved as if I hadn't heard my father and went up to my room and wept. I was considered an invalid or someone considered a liability with little or nothing to contribute.

As soon as I surrendered my life to Jesus in 1989, however, the asthma condition disappeared. My recurrent wheezing stopped, and I had no need for the perennial inhalers I carried around.

My formerly invalid position soon became an invaluable one as my siblings and parents relied on me to ensure things made it to completion in the family.

I rose to the top of my profession and became a storehouse for surplus and solution distribution. God took me from invalid to invaluable and from scarcity to surplus.

What you despise goes, and what you desire grows.

Chapter Three

Despising the Shame

Looking unto Jesus the author and finisher of our faith; who for the joy that was set before him endured the cross, despising the shame, and is set down at the right hand of the throne of God.
—Hebrews 12:2

Believers in Christ have mistaken shame for pity. They substitute one for the other, expecting their shame to evoke God's pity. On the contrary, walking in shame attracts evil and stops God's goodness from flowing into their lives.

Jesus understood the difference. At the garden of Gethsemane, where He was faced with the choice of dying on the cross in shame or calling legions of angels to eliminate all opposition and transition Him to heaven in glory, He chose the former.

He died a shameful death but despised the shame therein. Galatians 3:14 says, "Cursed is every one that hangs on a tree." The death on the cross was a shameful and cursed existence, but rather than excuse it, Jesus condemned it rather than condoned it. He died a shameful death, despising the shame so the body of Christ could live shamelessly every day of our lives. He desires for us not just to live shame free but also to despise or oppose shame anywhere we see it.

To Tolerate Is to Be Troubled Later

You are not called to tolerate shame or mediocre living but to rebuke and reject it. What many in today's church tolerate is despised by Jesus. Their tolerance becomes their trouble in the future.

Jesus did not tolerate the commercialization or circus charade going on in the holy temple of His day as so many Christians are wont to do. He stood up, destroyed their goods, and dared their protagonists' reprisals (Mark 11:15–17). He cursed a fig tree for not performing (Mark 11:14) and rattled the religious elite of his day by healing a man with a withered hand on the Sabbath (Mark 3:1–4).

Our code of conduct as Christians is to save the lost at all cost but despise their sin. Jude 23 says, "Save [others] with fear, pulling them out of the fire; hating even the garment spotted by the flesh."

Shame Starts Small

Nobody started as a drunkard; drunkards all started with one glass, and so does shame. What you tolerate today becomes the monster you face tomorrow if you do not nip it in the bud.

Jesus taught his disciples to "beware of the leaven of the Pharisees and of Herod" (Mark 8:15) because "a little leaven leaveneth the whole lump" (Galatians 5:9). If you do not stop sin, it will inevitably stop you at some point. It may be a private habit or indoor indiscretion now, but that shameful attitude and action will eventually snowball into a public calamity if you tolerate it. The wise man advised us in Songs of Solomon 2:15 to "take us the foxes, the little foxes, that spoil the vines for our vines have tender grapes."

Brother Charles: Ashamed and Afraid

In my six years of high school, we had one student obtain all the top positions at the end of every test, exam, or screening. Except once. Brother Charles, as he was famously called, stopped the machinery of this undisputed academic leader and topped our class in one test.

Unfortunately, that was the last thing Charles topped. To fit in with the high school society around him and not be considered queer by his peers, he started visiting prostitutes and engaging in sexually erotic activities. This formerly studious boy who would normally read sixteen hours a day started spending more time at brothels and bars. He hung around with the wrong group of teenagers, and they influenced him negatively.

At the time of our final exams, he was so disoriented mentally, spiritually, and physically that he couldn't take the exams. He failed high school, couldn't enter college, and at one point was placed in a mental health asylum for rehab.

Psalm 11:3 says, "If the foundations be destroyed what can the righteous do?" Charles had his foundations distorted by worldly wiles and satanic schemes. His prodigious talent ended up on the dustheap of history. That would have never happened if he had not been afraid of what people would say and feared God instead.

PART II

Altars: Altered or Alert?

You were born an original;
Don't die a copy.

Chapter Four

Awkward Altar

Know ye not that ye are the temple of God, and that the Spirit of God dwelleth in you? If any man defile the temple of God, him shall God destroy; for the temple of God is holy, which temple ye are.
—1 Corinthians 3:16–17

Two separate schools of thought seem to dominate the Christian landscape. They consist of ascetics, who seek to combine different forms of belief or practice, and the community of believers, who look to the Word of God and the Holy Spirit for direction.

True to type, ascetics mix idolatry from several false religions and Christianity instead of letting the finished work of Christ abide. For example, some erroneously believe they must touch or hold an apparition, clothing, or altar to make contact with God. Jesus addressed them in Matthew 23:18–19.

> Whosoever shall swear by the altar, it is nothing but whosoever swears by the gift that is upon it, he is guilty. Ye fools and blind for whether is greater, the gift, or the altar that sanctifies the gift?

Undue emphasis has been placed on a physical place to sanctify or cause a change when the Christian is a mobile altar and a readily available change agent. You shouldn't be looking for change elsewhere but be the change your world requires. Romans 12:1 adjures us to "present our bodies a living sacrifice, holy, acceptable unto God, which is your reasonable service."

Old Testament versus New Testament Altars

The altar in the Old Testament was an ark made of acacia wood and covered with gold (Exodus 25:10–11). It was 3 3/4 feet long by 2 1/4 feet wide and 2 1/4 feet high. It was an inanimate object and a symbol of God's presence in Israel. In Exodus 25:22, God said,

> I will meet with thee, and I will commune with thee from above the mercy seat, from between the two cherubims which are upon the ark of the testimony, of all things which I will give thee in commandment unto the children of Israel.

In the New Testament, God made the church (you and I) altars of God. We are His entry and exit point to the world and serve as a bridge that connects others with the God of all flesh.

While the altars were served by a genealogy of priests called the Levites, God "hath made us kings and priests unto God" (Revelation 1:6) to serve as living altars to our God. Our lives, not the sacrifice of bulls and goats, are what we offer on our altars as a sweet-smelling savor to Him because of the once and forever perfecting act of Jesus on the cross.

Anointing Upon or Anointing Within

The New Testament anointing is not upon the altar, as they had in the Old Testament (Leviticus 8:0–11), but within the believer. In 1 John 2:27a, we read, "The anointing which ye have received of him abides in you, and ye need not that any man teach you."

The new anointing is not found in exotic oil mixtures or powerful incenses or their smells, as was the case in the Old Testament (Exodus 30:22–38) but in the power of the Holy Spirit. Unfortunately, the New Testament church has abrogated its responsibility to be God's altar. It has instead made church buildings or its leaders its prayer altars when it has direct access to God via the blood of Jesus.

Prayer does not require a portfolio-carrying prophet or a power-packed program to be answered. You are God's altar, and just as He answered by fire when Solomon or Elijah raised an altar (2 Chronicles 7:1; 1 Kings 18:38 respectively), God will hear you.

As the altar of David was needed to stop the onslaught of a ravenous plague in Israel (2 Samuel 24:25), so can you stand for your family, church, and nation with heavenly results. That altar of David eventually became the temple of God built by Solomon (2 Chronicles 3:1), and so will your life be transformed as you pray for others.

The prayers of the saints are our most powerful armament and cannot be "outsourced" to someone or something. The awkward altar is why the power of prayer has been relegated to meal time and church time instead of what God intentioned—all time. He wants us to "pray without ceasing" (1 Thessalonians 5:17) and that "men pray every where, lifting up holy hands, without wrath and doubting" (1 Timothy 2:8).

My Altar Experience

On my wedding day in Enugu, Nigeria, it began to drizzle. I was outside the church taking pictures when the first drops splashed on my dark-grey tuxedo. It would not have mattered except for the fact that my wife and I had planned our outdoor tent wedding with complementary perfect weather. We were expecting at least two thousand festive and gaily dressed individuals, and we didn't want the rain to be a deterrent.

As the rain dabbed my face, I called upon the God of all the earth and decreed for the rain to stop in the name of Jesus. Within minutes, the rains ceased and the sky was once again clear.

At his welcome address at the reception, the chairman called those initial rains a "shower of blessings." In my view, it was God's intervention that saved the wedding reception.

It would have been impossible, however, if the altar had been altered and not used as a place of power to reach God and change the earth. Like Elijah, we hold the earth ransom with our altar-approaching, earthquake-evoking, and spirit-saturating prayers when we know we are God's altar and the change agent for our community.

When you focus on the opposition, you lose your position.

Chapter Five

Alert Altars

*For the Lord G*OD *will help me; therefore shall I not be confounded: therefore have I set my face like a flint, and I know that I shall not be ashamed.*
—Isaiah 50:7

An alert altar is one that abides by divine orders and instructions. In the Old Testament, God told Moses, "as it was shewed thee in the mount, so shall they make it" (Exodus 27:8).

This lack of attention to divine details has robbed the church of its glory at the altar. Instead of glory, there is a mishmash of shame from shortcuts and delay in doing things without divine order.

Before being introduced to Him, as one who despised the shame of the cross in Hebrews 12:2, we are asked to "look unto Jesus the author and finisher of our faith."

Your sight of God determines your might on earth. In 2 Corinthians 3:18, we read, "We all with open face beholding as in a glass the glory of the Lord, are changed into the same image from glory to glory, even as by the Spirit of the Lord."

Life is not a cookbook that allows you to cook and look away but a continuous crucible that demands a permanent looking at the Word to survive and thrive. James 1:25 says, "Whoso looks into the perfect law of liberty, and continues therein, he being not a forgetful hearer, but a doer of the work, this man shall be blessed in his deed."

Strange Fire

Leviticus 10:1–2 says,

> Nadab and Abihu, the sons of Aaron, took either of them his censer, and put fire therein, and put incense thereon, and offered strange fire before the LORD, which he commanded them not. And there went out fire from the LORD, and devoured them, and they died before the LORD.

One infringement against God's Word cost Abihu and Nadab their lives at the altar. When God's Word is contravened, destruction is inevitable, even if it is at the altar. The altar is not a place for loss of focus but for following the Word of God purposely.

They were offering sacrifices and doing their priestly chores, but because they did so not according to divine order, they were consumed. It is not enough to just claim church attendance or religious routines as your escape route from shame; you must follow God's divine manual.

In the parable of the five foolish and five wise virgins, Jesus warns us, "Watch therefore, for ye know neither the day nor the hour wherein the Son of man cometh to watch therefore" (Matthew 25:13). Though all ten were virgins, five were alert with light in their lamps when the bridegroom came, while the five foolish virgins missed the marriage supper of the Lamb because they had no light or focus.

The psalmist said in Psalm 34:5, "They looked unto him, and were lightened and their faces were not ashamed." One wrong step can lead to a lifetime of shame. Be alert at the altar of life, and look before you leap. Those who do so are assured by God of a shame-free existence.

True Worship

True worship starts when the veil of religion is shred and you focus solely on Jesus. In John 4, Jesus met a beleaguered and ashamed Samaritan woman. She had come to the well at midday because she was too ashamed of her past to herald the crowd of women. According to Jesus, she "worshipped [what she] knows not what ... but the hour cometh, and now is, when the true worshippers shall worship the

Father in spirit and in truth for the Father seeks such to worship him" (John 4:22–23).

This woman is a mirror of many in the church today. Like her, they are beset by conflicting dogmas and doctrines and don't know the God of the Bible. They live in a state of shame and a canopy of confusion, hoping for a better tomorrow that never arrives.

Their problem is lack of perception and alertness. Rather than serving a spoon-fed Christianity, the church must grow into maturity by taking off the veil of religion and seeing Jesus with an open face.

Arriving in Arcadia

I arrived in Arcadia, Louisiana, with a sense of conviction and fulfillment. I knew God had called me to Louisiana, and I was determined to completely fulfill the purpose God had sent my wife and me to Arcadia for.

Even before my clinic took off, I started a monthly prayer meeting named Holy Ghost Night in this rustic, rural town. As we grew, our impact was beginning to be felt, and widespread commotion was taking place in the spiritual world. Long-held ancient doors and gates began to challenge us, and we had negative comments spread around town about us. Unfavorable calls and comments at my office designed to scare me began making the rounds, but I stayed focused and alert.

When the conundrum raised by some contending parties got blown out of proportion, I was let go by my head office, and I relocated to another practice in South Louisiana. Three years later, I still get nostalgic phone calls and texts from people asking us to return.

By God's grace, we raised an altar in that own that was alert and not altered. We believe that altar still speaks today because it was raised according to divine instruction and not according to human whims and caprices.

PART III

STEPS to the Altar

- **S**hame
- **T**actics
- **E**mptiness
- **P**owerlessness
- **S**uperficiality

God never makes trash;
He makes only treasures.

Chapter Six

Shame

Neither shalt thou go up by steps unto mine altar, that thy
nakedness (or shame) be not discovered thereon.
—Exodus 20:26

An epidemic of insecurity, intimidation, and feelings of inferiority, otherwise called shame, is curtailing the body of Christ from fulfilling its potential. The priest was advised to avoid steps in the Old Testament (Exodus 20:26) if he wanted to avoid shame at the altar.

The ultimate reason this chosen generation is living ashamed at the altar instead of basking in God's glory is that many have permitted shame and put away God's glory from their lives. Romans 9:33 says, "I lay in Sion a stumblingstone and rock of offence [which is Jesus] and whosoever believeth on him shall not be ashamed."

Your life is designed for glory, not shame. It was designed for faith, not fear, and for assurance, not assumption. If the Old Testament ministration of God to Moses, according to 2 Corinthians 3:7, was glorious, "How shall not the ministration of the spirit be rather glorious?" (2 Corinthians 3:8).

Not Ashamed

Paul declared in Romans 1:16, "I am not ashamed of the gospel of Christ for it is the power of God unto salvation to every one that believeth." Where there is shame, there is no faith, and where there is no faith, prayer is ineffective.

Hebrews 11:6 says, "Without faith it is impossible to please him for he that comes to God must believe that he is, and that he is a rewarder of them that diligently seek him."

The spirit of shame erodes the altar of its potency because there is an absence of boldness and confidence in approaching God. Hebrews 4:16 says, "Let us therefore come boldly unto the throne of grace, that we may obtain mercy, and find grace to help in time of need."

The altar of prayer is not a place of shame but a place for boldness. James 5:16–18 records that Elijah changed the face of the Israelite kingdom by prayer: "The effectual fervent prayer of a righteous man avails much [for] Elias was a man subject to like passions as we are, and he prayed earnestly that it might not rain: and it rained not."

He intimidated kings (1 Kings 21:20), changed the course of nature (1 Kings 17:1), and spoke a word that God established (1 Kings 18:45) because he was earnest, fervent, and bold in prayer. Shame is the great robber of the twenty-first-century church. Too many hold onto their pecuniary perspectives and miss divine directives that could catapult them into glory because of past shame.

With as many as half of African-American men going to jail at one time or another,[5] and as many as a fourth of US females raped or physically assaulted in their lifetimes, shame has preponderance in the US population. It is a canker in America's social fiber and must be radically excised by Christ to save its victims.

Bye Bye to Shame

Confidence in God is not motivational hype but a kingdom necessity. Jesus did not leave us here to consume or be consumed but to conquer. He commanded us to "occupy till he comes" (Luke 19:13).

The word used for *occupy* in Luke 19:13 means "to practice repeatedly and habitually." We must not become so conversant with shame or complacent about glory that we fail to identify it and eliminate it from our midst.

The synonym of *shame* is *disgrace*. Anywhere there is shame, grace has been rejected. Without the grace of God, shame is inevitable.

Romans 3:23 says, "For all have sinned and come short of the glory of God."

You don't have to settle for shame. Reach out for the glory of God. Glory is not just our destiny, as stated in Romans 8:30; it should be our destination or residence wherever we go. The glory of God is where we should always reside.

Jeremiah 17:12 says, "A glorious high throne from the beginning is the place of our sanctuary," and Isaiah 62:3 says, "Thou shall be a crown of glory in the hand of the LORD."

Suffering and Smiling

The Gospels never indicate we would not suffer because we became Christians but ask us to suffer gloriously instead of shamefully. In 2 Corinthians 4:17, the apostle Paul said, "For our light affliction, which is but for a moment, worketh for us a far more exceeding and eternal weight of glory."

He wasn't just sitting and shamefully waiting for the great bye and bye to take him home; he chose to glorify God in the midst of his afflictions by pursuing God's objectives. Many in the twenty-first-century church have, instead, embraced a "suffer and be shamed" doctrine that is alien to the gospel and erroneously set up on unbiblical foundations.

It is not what you go through but how you go through it that determines your outcome. The church needs an attitude shift from suffering and being shamed toward suffering and smiling instead. In 1 Peter 4:16, we read, "Yet if any man suffer as a Christian, let him not be ashamed; but let him glorify God on this behalf."

Paul remained confident, even in chains, because he knew who won in the end—Jesus Christ and His body, the church. Stand therefore with your shoulders squared, your head held high, and your eyes straight ahead in spite of every possible denigration of your reputation because you know the final outcome is victory for Christians.

More Royal Than a Rolls-Royce

The Rolls-Royce was first built in 1904 by Henry Royce. In 1906, production increased after a merger with Charles Roll, who owned a car dealership and invested a substantial amount of funds.

The Rolls-Royce had a nine-cylinder engine with low-level sound dynamics. It had two core principles: silence even at 140 miles per hour and a sense of immutability that defied even mythology.

Two statements made popular by Rolls-Royce highlight these two cardinal points. The first statement placed on the factory grounds read, "Beware—Silent Cars," and the second statement read, "A Rolls-Royce never breaks down; it only fails to proceed."

A famous aristocrat once had a faulty Rolls-Royce in Paris. He called London for the repair team, and someone promised a quick intervention and resolution.

The next morning, after noting no obvious mechanical work on the car, he called London, complaining that no one had come to repair the Rolls-Royce as promised. To his utter shock, the receptionist denied ever having a report of a broken-down Rolls-Royce in Paris and replied adamantly, "Rolls-Royce cars never break down."

However, the hotel porter told him some men had discreetly worked on the car overnight. After careful inspection, he noted the car had been fixed and was ready for the road. He called London asking for his bill, but the Rolls-Royce office replied, "Rolls-Royce cars never break down." No bill was required.

Our royalty as kings and priests of our God (Revelation 1:6) is greater than that of the Rolls-Royce. We should accord ourselves with more royalty and have zero shame time because our maker is God, not man.

We are God's reflection on the earth; consequently, what the world sees of us is what they think of Him. As with a Rolls-Royce, do they think of glory when they see us, or are we repeatedly shamed artifacts that have no resemblance to their Maker?

If you are not inspired, you will soon expire.

Chapter Seven

Tactics

*Joshua built an altar unto the L*ORD* God ... an altar of whole stones,*
over which no man hath lift up any iron and they offered thereon
*burnt offerings unto the L*ORD*, and sacrificed peace offerings.*
- Joshua 8:30–31

The word *tactics* means "the deployment and directing of weapons and warriors to effective maneuvers against an enemy." In the formation of the altar, God warned against the use of man-made tools or tactics because they would bring shame, not glory. In Exodus 20:25, the Bible says "And if thou wilt make me an altar of stone, thou shall not build it of hewn stone for if thou lift up thy tool upon it, thou hast polluted (or shamed) it."

Tactics are an accumulation of man-made steps to solve demonic problems, and no matter how hard people try, they will fail. The word *whole* used in Joshua 8:31 means "secure" in the original Hebrew and signifies that a true altar is secure in God and will not compromise with lesser gods. Jeremiah 17:5–6 says,

> Thus saith the Lord, cursed be the man that trusteth in man, and maketh flesh his arm, and whose heart departeth from the LORD. For he shall be like the heath in the desert, and shall not see when good cometh; but shall inhabit the parched places in the wilderness, in a salt land and not inhabited.

Regardless of lineage or pedigree, only what God says will stand. God will not share His glory with any person (Isaiah 42:8) no matter how wise, intelligent, or astute he or she may be. God is God all by Himself, and there is none other.

Shame Starts with Self

The worst work a man can do is self-work. Jesus said, "For without me ye can do nothing" (John 15:5b). Life is an empty shell and a cacophony of nothingness without the presence of Jesus.

The best plans and the most resourceful ideas will succeed only if God approves of them. In Lamentations 3:37, the prophet asked, "Who is he that saith, and it cometh to pass, when the Lord commandeth it not?" The psalmist said, "Commit thy way unto the Lord; trust also in him and He shall bring it to pass" (Psalm 37:5). This command does not forfeit the benefit of plans, but it asks that all such plans be made under guidance of the Holy Spirit. There is nothing wrong with plans, but without God, the best of plans are void of substance.

Proverbs 3:5–6 says, "Lean not unto thine own understanding. In all thy ways acknowledge him, and he shall direct thy paths." Until you live without waiting for human interpretation or interruption, you haven't started living like a whole stone.

Made in Heaven, Delivered on Earth

Believers are not earthly but heavenly. Jesus said, "He that cometh from above is above all: he that is of the earth is earthly, and speaketh of the earth. He that cometh from heaven is above all" (John 3:31).

As long as men concern themselves with earthly tactics and the wisdom of the world, they will be bereft of supernatural impact. Philippians 3:19b–20 says, "[Their] end is destruction, whose God is their belly, and whose glory is in their shame, who mind earthly things. For our conversation is in heaven."

Heaven rules the earth, and there is no physical problem without a spiritual solution. Matthew 18:18 says, "Whatsoever ye shall bind on earth shall be bound in heaven and whatsoever ye shall loose on earth shall be loosed in heaven."

Christians are heavenly citizens on an earthly sojourn for our King, and they cannot be more concerned with earthly matters than His heavenly vision. This world's wisdom is "earthly, sensual [and] devilish" (James 3:15), but the wisdom of God is "pure, peaceable, gentle, easy to be in treated, full of mercy and good fruits, without partiality, and without hypocrisy" (James 3:17).

Wisdom Works

Walking in divine wisdom guarantees glory and eliminates shame in a Christian's life. Proverbs 3:35 says, "The wise shall inherit glory; but shame shall be the promotion of fools." Walking in wisdom stimulates success as assuredly as a fire will produce burning.

Wisdom is the foolproof success key for birthing a breakthrough, and according to Jesus, it is justified by its children (Luke 7:35). In Matthew 7:24, a wise man is described as "whosoever hears these sayings [of Jesus] and does them."

Until a man or woman becomes a doer of God's Word, he or she cannot walk in divine wisdom. The wisdom we need is not the know-how of Silicon Valley or the resourcefulness of Wall Street; we need the influence of the Word of God that produces true godly and life-changing wisdom.

Traditions, Tactics, or Trusting God

Until you come under the authority of the Word of God, you will be continually ashamed. In 2 Samuel 22:35–36, we learn, "He teaches my hands to war; so that a bow of steel is broken by mine arms. Thou hast also given me the shield of thy salvation: and thy gentleness hath made me great."

You cannot call upon God with a tactical mind and a traditional spirit and manifest His glory on earth. Psalm 119:39 says, "Turn away my reproach which I fear: for thy judgments are good."

There must be no preconceived ideas or self-made plans when you come to God's altar. In Exodus 10:26, Moses told Pharaoh, "There shall not an hoof be left behind; for thereof must we take to serve the Lord our God; and we know not with what we must serve the Lord, until we come thither."

A free spirit is the antidote for a shameful spirit. Tactics and traditions are stifling spirits that crush the liberty Jesus came to give us. Jesus said, "Thus have ye made the commandment of God of none effect by your tradition" (Matthew 15:6).

The solution to shame is rejecting tactics and traditions and trusting God wholeheartedly; 2 Corinthians 3:17–18 says,

> Where the Spirit of the Lord is, there is liberty. But we all, with open face beholding as in a glass the glory of the Lord, are changed into the same image from glory to glory, even as by the Spirit of the Lord.

It takes liberty in the spirit to stir up increased levels of glory in our lives. Let go and let God. He will remove shame and multiply glory exponentially, but first you must release yourself to him. In Matthew 16:24,27, Jesus said, "If any man will come after me, let him deny himself, and take up his cross, and follow me … [and] the Son of man shall come in the glory of his Father with his angels; and reward every man according to his works."

My Patient with Breast Cancer

Mrs. A. S. came into the prayer meeting downcast and with shoulders drooped. She had just returned from a doctor's appointment. His diagnosis spelled possible doom; a mammogram suggested she had breast cancer. Her doctor suggested a follow up with a surgeon and a biopsy for confirmation.

It was in that state of mind that A. S. walked into the Holy Ghost Night of April 2013. It was a first-time visit, but it would not be her last. A chance invitation had aroused her interest knowing at that point that only God could change her story.

While prayer and ministry were in process, the visiting minister asked A. S. to come forward for prayer. He told her by divine revelation that she had just been diagnosed with a disease but that God was going to heal her.

A. S. was stunned. Having been raised in a traditional Christian background and knowing full well no one could have informed the minister about her condition, she received the words of God with full expectation of a miracle.

Twenty-four hours later, following her visit to a surgeon, she experienced her miracle firsthand. The surgeon told her that repeat mammograms showed no indication of cancer.

He could find no suitable scientific explanations for this difference. A. S. has had no return of symptoms since then, and she is walking whole and in health since. She attributes the anointing of the Holy Spirit, not human understanding, as the source of her twenty-four-hour miracle.

God sends no one away empty *except those who are* full *of themselves.*

Chapter Eight

Emptiness

It is not good to eat much honey: so for men to search their
own glory is not glory. He that hath no rule over his own spirit
is like a city that is broken down, and without walls.
—Proverbs 25:27–28

One of the crucial causes of shame in the church today is emptiness. The word *empty* is defined as not filled, containing nothing. That is not, however, what God intended for a Christian. A Christian is designed to live a full, not an empty life. Jesus said, "The thief cometh not, but for to steal, and to kill, and to destroy: I am come that they might have life, and that they might have it more abundantly" (John 10:10).

The ignominy so many Christians experience starts with not being full of God's life-giving spirit but rather becoming full of themselves. Galatians 6:3 says, "If a man thinks himself to be something, when he is nothing, he deceives himself."

Pride or being full of self causes inevitable shame. Hosea 4:7 says, "As they were increased, so they sinned against me: therefore will I change their glory into shame." The reason so many start in glory and end in shame is that they were empty of God and full of self.

What happens to a self-adulating and vainglorious individual is certain shame. Proverbs 11:2 says, "When pride cometh, then cometh shame: but with the lowly is wisdom." Emptiness is preceded by pride, and pride is always followed by a fall. Proverbs 16:18 says, "Pride goeth before destruction, and an haughty spirit before a fall."

Saul and Shame

Saul died a shameful death on the mountains of Gilboa. In 2 Samuel 1:21, we read,

> Ye mountains of Gilboa, let there be no dew, neither let there be rain, upon you, nor fields of offerings: for there the shield of the mighty is vilely cast away, the shield of Saul, as though he had not been anointed with oil.

He fell not to an enemy's sword or a marksman's arrow but to pride. In 1 Samuel 15:17, prophet Samuel asked Saul, "When thou was little in thine own sight, was thou not made the head of the tribes of Israel, and the Lord anointed thee king over Israel?"

He died in ignominy because he was full of himself and empty of God. Rather than consult God, he turned to the occult (1 Samuel 28:7–9). He died on the same day and in the same battle as his son and crown prince Jonathan. He was uncelebrated and unheralded because his pride brought shame.

If you want to live a life of sustainable glory, you must first be willing to put on the garments of humility. As 1 Peter 5:6 says, "Humble yourselves therefore under the mighty hand of God, that he may exalt you in due time."

Daily Manna

Moses instructed the Israelites "let no man leave of it [manna] till the morning" (Exodus 16:19). When they attempted to live on yesterday's manna, maggots appeared in it (Exodus 16:20). Christians cannot live on yesterday's manna today. It takes a daily infilling of His presence to sustain God's glory on the earth. Like the early disciples, we do not depend on a single upper room Pentecostal experience but are continually filled with the Holy Spirit daily (see Acts 4:31).

Lamentations 3:22–23 says, "His compassions fail not [for] they are new every morning [and] great is thy faithfulness." God wants the church to go from strength to strength (Psalm 84:7), from glory to glory (2 Corinthians 3:17), and from faith to faith. He punishes complacency and spiritual indifference that comes from a lack of pursuing God. In Zephaniah 1:12–13, God said,

> I will search Jerusalem with candles, and punish the men that are settled on their lees: that say in their heart, The Lord will not do good, neither will he do evil. Therefore their goods shall become a booty, and their houses a desolation.

Ashes on the Altar

Vanity or the emptiness of the past is what causes shame at the altar. Some people hold onto the past instead of pressing on into the future, as Paul did (Philippians 3:10–14). The way Paul obliterated shame from his life was by focusing on his glorious future and forgetting his beleaguered past.

In Philippians 1:20, Paul said, "According to my earnest expectation and my hope, that in nothing I shall be ashamed, but that with all boldness, as always, so now also Christ shall be magnified in my body, whether it be by life, or by death."

Expectation and hope are the birthplace of shamelessness in life. Romans 5:5 says, "Hope makes not ashamed; because the love of God is shed abroad in our hearts by the Holy Ghost which is given unto us."

Looking in the rearview mirror of life is a sine qua non for a wasted and shameful destiny. In Leviticus 1:16, when the priests were asked to dispose of the ashes, God commanded them, "Pluck away his crop [dung] with his feathers, and cast it beside the altar on the east part, by the place of the ashes."

The ashes on your altar, including the shame of rejection, hurt, or abandonment are condemned to the dunghills of life and have no place on your altar. Don't recycle the past; instead, accelerate into your future by forgetting your past and considering it as detestable as dung.

Instead of Wind, Bring Forth Word

In Isaiah 26:18, Israel said to God, "We have as it were brought forth wind; we have not wrought any deliverance in the earth [and] neither have the inhabitants of the world fallen."

An empty life lacks the substance of the Word of God. Many believers make wind instead of word because they lose focus on their destinies. In 1 Samuel 12:21, we read, "Turn ye not aside: for then should ye go after vain things, which cannot profit nor deliver; for they are vain."

Distraction is the Devil's biggest attraction in sabotaging a Christian's destiny. Paul described it as beating air or running uncertainly. In 1 Corinthians 9:26–27, Paul said,

> I run, not as uncertainly [and] so fight I, not as one that beats the air but I keep under my body, and bring it into subjection lest that by any means, when I have preached to others, I myself should be a castaway.

When the Devil wants to stop your vision, he gives you another one or makes you focus on your past. The Word of God is your firm foundation and a sure platform for escaping shame.

Third Day and the Suicidal Kid

A young man in New Jersey was young, capricious, and wanted to end it all. He felt a failure in life and thought the best way out was to kill himself. He loaded his gun and drove as deep into the dense woods as he could. Before he shot himself, however, he wanted to listen one last time to his favorite radio show. Unfortunately, because of how far he was from modernity, he could not pick up any radio signal except one.

It was a Christian radio station in New Jersey;' it was playing a song from Third Day's album "Born Again." As he heard the lyrics, he confessed his sins to Jesus and asked for forgiveness.

He drove out of the forest and back home, fully restored. He gave his life to Jesus because he had heard a song proclaiming the healing love of Jesus' name. At an amphitheater in New Jersey, during a Third Day concert, this young man came forward and shared his testimony.

His empty life had been filled by the love and life of God that never stops filling. He encountered God and saw his emptiness reversed and God's fullness awakened in him and through him.

When the immoveable meets the unstoppable, the lesser power must bow.

Chapter Nine

Powerlessness

I am not ashamed of the gospel of Christ: for it is the power
of God unto salvation to everyone that believeth.
—Romans 1:16

A powerless church is the reason for the shame in the body of Christ today. In the early church,

> great fear came upon all the church, and upon as many as heard these things (because) by the hands of the apostles were many signs and wonders wrought among the people and of the rest durst no man join himself to them but the people magnified them. (Acts 5:11–13)

The presence of the Holy Spirit equips the believer with the power of heaven (Acts 1:8). Until you walk in that power, you cannot walk away from shame. Power is your guarantee of shamelessness in life. Isaiah 37:27 says, "Their inhabitants were of small power [and so they were] dismayed and confounded."

When Job walked in the anointing of the Holy Spirit, shame was nonexistent. Job 29:20–21 says his "glory was fresh in him and his bow renewed in his hand [as] unto him men gave ear and waited, and kept silence at his counsel." Until we stay with the power of God, there is no exit from shame. Zephaniah 3:17–19 says,

The Lord thy God in the midst of thee is mighty; He will save, he will rejoice over thee with joy; he will rest in his love, he will joy over thee with singing [and] at that time undo all that afflict thee and save her that halts. I will get them praise and fame in every land where they have been put to shame.

Samson and Shame

Samson had taken God for granted and had given the secret of his strength to Delilah. In Judges 16:19, we read, "She made him sleep upon her knees; and she called for a man, and caused him to shave off the seven locks of his head; and she began to afflict him, and his strength went from him."

He woke up after Delilah had shaved him, expecting to walk into his usual power but was bereft of it. Judges 16:20 says Samson "awoke out of his sleep, and said, I will go out as at other time before, and shake myself and he wist not that the Lord was departed from him."

Eventually, Samson had his eyes gouged out and was made to grind maize at the Philistine's mill (Judges 16:21). A man once feared and revered as a great judge of Israel had lost his sight and might to laissez-faire living. The power of God had become customary and he took it for granted. He trifled with the Holy Spirit and ended life dying with his enemies in shame and disgrace.

Signs Should Follow You, Not Shame

Mark 16:17a says, "These signs shall follow them that believe." God did not promise believers shame but a plethora of signs and wonders.

The early disciples were timid, fearful, and filled with shame until the Holy Spirit came upon them in Acts 1. In John 20:19, the disciples had "the doors shut [because] they were assembled for fear of the Jews." They felt they had lost their champion when Jesus died and felt disillusioned and vulnerable.

After the baptism of the Holy Spirit, however, the disciples healed the paralytic at the gate by the name of Jesus Christ and were arraigned before the rulers and elders of Israel (Acts 4:4–19). They were not ashamed of the gospel at this juncture, and even their high-ranking audience noted "the boldness of Peter and John, and perceived that they were unlearned and ignorant men [and so] marveled" (Acts 4:13).

The difference between the Peter who denied Jesus in Matthew 26:69–72 and the Peter who spoke amidst ten thousand and more people on the day of Pentecost was the power of the Holy Spirit.

Shame exits when the Spirit of God enters. The Spirit of God is the power of God, and you cannot be simultaneously ashamed and empowered with the Spirit. After their shameless declaration of the gospel, "they prayed [and] the place was shaken where they were assembled together and they were all filled with the Holy Ghost, and spoke the word of God with boldness" (Acts 4:31).

The Frozen Chosen

Shame will follow the "frozen" even if they are chosen. If you do not renew the fullness of the Holy Spirit in your life daily, you will end up ashamed and with non renewed strength and an un refreshed anointing. You will be among the "frozen chosen," believers who start in the Spirit but end up in the flesh. For example, Eli deferred to his sons more than to the Word of God. He turned a blind eye to their whoredom and the idolatry they perpetrated (1 Samuel 3:13) and as a result, "The glory departed from Israel [as] the ark of God was taken" (1 Samuel 4:13).

When the Israelites walked into the territory of the Philistines, there was the "noise of a great shout in the camp of the Hebrews" (1 Samuel 4:6), but there was no presence of the Spirit. They had the posturing but lacked the presence of God, and so consequently they suffered shame.

The aftereffect of this cosmetic and crass Christianity was Ichabod, whose name meant "the glory has departed from Israel." Eli lost his family's future and fortune to powerless living. He, his sons, and his daughters-in-law died on the same day and sentenced their legacy to a lifetime of shame (1 Samuel 2:32–34) because they lacked the presence or fire of the Holy Spirit (1 Samuel 3:3).

Job 32:8 says, "there is a spirit in man and the inspiration of the Almighty gives them understanding." The glory is in direct proportion to your inspiration by the Holy Spirit. If you refuse to be inspired, you will surely expire.

Supernatural Spiritual Secrets

Your life is not designed to be a shell but a shell shock to the world around you. You are called to walk in the footsteps of Jesus and do greater works than He did. John 14:12 says, "He that believeth on me, the works that I do shall he do also; and greater works than these shall he do; because I go unto my Father," and 1 John 4:17 says, "As he is, so are we in this world."

Supernatural encounters with God are not start-stop relationships but a continuous communion with divinity through the power of the Holy Spirit. Psalm 91:1 says, "He that dwells in the secret place of the most High shall abide under the shadow of the Almighty."

The secret place of the most high refers to a lifestyle of studying, meditating, and praying without ceasing. When you make God's presence your utmost desire, He will give you your highest delights.

We should have the Upper Room experience on a daily basis if we want to live above the umbrella of shame. Isaiah 28:5–6 says,

> The Lord of hosts [shall] be a crown of glory, [as] a diadem of beauty unto the residue of his people and for a spirit of judgment to him that sits in judgment and for strength to them that turn the battle to the gate.

Power Pass Power

I was a marked man. I had reported the longest-serving professor of anatomy to the authorities for conniving with his sons to divulge exam questions prior to exams. As a result, some of the lecturers wanted a piece of my hide for ridiculing their colleague. Some called it camaraderie, while others considered it a matter of collective interests, but I just needed the nightmare to end.

I soon realized that some of these lecturers had it in for me. Because my allegations had not been substantiated, I was compelled to take the anatomy exam again under the supervision of the same professor I had reported to the college provost. Friends of mine told me the professor I had reported had vowed to see me fail that exam. I studied, took the exam, and waited for the results.

I needed this course to continue with my clinical training, and failure was unthinkable. On the day of its release, there was an unprecedented three-to-four-hour delay in publishing the results.

At the end of the marathon examiners' meeting, the results were published. I passed and was celebrating on the streets when the dean of the pre clinical medical school accosted me and told me I had been responsible for the delay in the meeting. He told me that my results had been hotly debated and disputed with the professor I reported to the provost. He had insisted I fail the exam even though I had enough right answers to pass. Eventually, the dean of the medical school stood up for me and insisted I be given a pass in the course.

A few months later, a thorough investigation was carried out, and this overtly corrupt professor was dismissed. God's power overcame the demons of criminality and corruption in the department and made me a medical doctor today.

The greatest testimony is when those who know you best respect you most.

Chapter Ten

Superficiality

For the which cause I also suffer these things: nevertheless I am not
ashamed: for I know whom I have believed, and am persuaded that he is
able to keep that which I have committed unto him against that day.
—2 Timothy 1:12.

Shame, superficiality, and lack of substance have characterized the twenty-first- century church. Rather than look for substance, the church has looked at shadows, and rather than go for depth in God, it has being dillydallying at God's instructions.

Psalm 42:7 says, "Deep calleth unto deep at the noise of thy waterspouts." The depths of God are reserved for those who go deep with God. The treasure-house of heaven is not found superficially or on surface-level Christianity but in depths of revelation with Him.

Isaiah 45:3 says, "I will give thee the treasures of darkness, and hidden riches of secret places, that thou may know that I, the Lord, which call thee by thy name, am the God of Israel."

The most precious elements on earth, such as gold, diamonds, ore, and even petroleum, are found by digging into the depths. Likewise, only the depths of God can give you the deepest desires of your heart.

Stop Shallow Living

Your shallow living is the reason you live in shame. It takes depth to attain glory and perseverance to live shamelessly. "It is the glory of God to conceal a thing but the honor of kings to search [it] out" (Proverbs 25:2). Where your glory lies is not in the shallow waters of convenience or custom but in the deep place of God. When Peter needed to make a catch after toiling all day, Jesus told him, "Launch out into the deep, and let down your nets for a draught" (Luke 5:4). Peter's net-breaking catch did not come from superficial fishing that used man-made formulas and criteria. It came by taking God at his Word and going deep with Him.

In Hebrews 5:12, the Lord said, "When the time ye ought to be teachers, ye have need that one teach you again which be the first principles of the oracles of God; and are become such as have need of milk, and not of strong meat."

A lack of maturity due to spineless and weak-kneed Christianity is the reason there is a preponderance of shame in the church today. Psalm 102:16 says "When the LORD shall build up Zion, he shall appear in his glory."

Waters You Can't Walk Over

The prophet Ezekiel chronicled a story of an overflowing river and its differing levels in Ezekiel 47. He said the Spirit brought him "out of the way of the gate northward, and led me about the way without unto the utter gate by the way that looketh eastward; and, behold, there ran out waters on the right side" (Ezekiel 47:2). The waters were shallow until the Spirit took him into "a river that he could not pass over for the waters were risen [as] ... a river that could not be passed over" (Ezekiel 47:5).

Staying in shallow water leaves you ashamed, but going into the deep brings out the life of God in you. In Ezekiel 47:8–9, those depths caused "the waters [to] be healed and ... every thing that lives [or] moves [and] whithersoever the rivers shall come, shall live."

Jesus said in John 7:38, "He that believeth on me, as the scripture hath said, out of his belly shall flow rivers of living waters." We must leave the surface and go for His substance to bring life to our generation.

Don't live a cosmetic Christianity but a charismatic Christianity that is empty of self and full of the power of the Holy Spirit. God is not a slot machine that you put a token into and expect instant results from. He is a God who desires your relationship, so stop being content with the superficial and go for substance.

Glorious Depths by Going Deeper

Shame is the result of superficial living. When Jesus saw the fig tree from afar, it gave the appearance of fruitfulness. Mark 11:13a says Jesus saw the "fig tree afar off having leaves [and] came, if haply, he might find any thing thereon."

The fig tree had no sustainable fruits, however, in spite of its superficial appearance of fruitfulness. Because of its superficiality, it was cursed by Jesus. Mark 11:13b-14 says, "When Jesus came to it, he found nothing but leaves, for the time of figs was not yet, And Jesus answered and said unto it, No man eat fruit of thee hereafter for ever."

All through the ages, deep thinkers have ruled. The wealthiest and most modern countries in the world are not necessarily the resource-rich countries such as Saudi Arabia or South Africa but the technologically advanced countries such as Japan and Germany. The latter emphasize mental advancements rather than physical possessions.

In the kingdom of God, the unseen rules the seen, and the spiritual always triumphs over the physical. In 2 Corinthians 4:18, we read, "While we look not at the things which are seen, but at the things which are not seen: for the things which are seen are temporal; but the things which are not seen are eternal."

Every physical problem has a spiritual solution, and we must attack the spiritual to solve the physical. To abrogate shame in the physical, you must eliminate porous, anemic, and lame Christianity in the spiritual. Until the church matures, it will not hear the Word from strong meat that changes you from shame to glory. Hebrews 5:13–14 says,

> Every one that useth milk is unskilful in the word of righteousness: for he is a babe. But strong meat belongeth to them that are of full age, even those who by reason of use have their senses exercised to discern both good and evil.

Turkanaland: Healed Foundations from Deep Depths

The people of Turkanaland, Kenya, have borne the brunt of famine and deprivation for decades as a result of lack of water. Their part of Kenya has a 37 percent malnutrition rate and 9.5 million people affected by the 2011 drought.

The desert conditions prevalent in Turkanaland affect cattle, farming, and humans. The average Turkanaland native walks at least ten miles daily to obtain water for basic needs and so leaves this northwestern enclave of Kenya short of suitable manpower for schools and education.

In 2012, French scientists commissioned by UNESCO began seismic studies looking for underground water or mineral reserves. At the same time, a Kenyan couple working in Louisiana (Sammy and Mary Murimi) began praying for the healing of Turkanaland.

The seismic studies uncovered five underground pools in Turkanaland, including a large one at Lotikipi, which is about the size of Rhode Island. Under it were 200 million cubic meters of fresh water. This underground aquifer is naturally replenished by rainfall at the rate of 1.2 million cubic meters per year. It is 330 meters below the surface and is projected to last at least seventy years.

This discovery has single-handedly changed the economy of the Turkanaland people. They now have borehole water access and, in no time, the farmland that had been subsistent and barely surviving will become irrigated and sustainable.

The healing of Turkanaland has turned those who were in the cold clutches of poverty into those with the most sought-after land in Kenya. The prayer of Sammy and Mary Murimi and other missionaries for the healing of the land came true, and Turkanaland will never be the same again. Truly, deep calls unto deep.

PART IV

The Seven Spirits of Shame

Satan is in the shame and blame game;
God is in the surplus and blessings bonanza.

Chapter Eleven

Satanic "Shamists"

*God hath not given us the spirit of fear but of power, and of love, and of a
sound mind. Be not thou therefore ashamed of the testimony of our Lord.*
—2 Timothy 1:7–8a

There are multitudes of Christians suffering in shame instead
of smiling and striving for the kingdom of God because they
have been deceived by the seven spirits of shame or satanic
"shamists" ravaging the world today.

These believers give into self-pity, low self-esteem, poor self-image
and walk in unmitigated shame instead of the unforgettable glory of
God. They have no expectation or hope because they are wallowing in
shame (Philippians 1:20) and so recover nothing glorious.

The Devil has come, "having great wrath, because he knows that
he hath but a short time" (Revelation 12:12). Shame is an arch weapon
of his in these last days because he knows that without boldness, you
can't come to the altar and receive grace, mercy, or help in your time
of need.

Hebrews 4:16 says, "Let us therefore come boldly unto the throne
of grace, that we may obtain mercy, and find grace to help in time of
need." Shame stops us from boldly approaching God's throne of grace
and limits our divine load of blessings.

Elijah's Exit

Elijah was God's battering ram that destroyed the enemies of God. He was used by God to single-handedly kill 450 prophets of Baal (1 Kings 18:40), push King Ahab to the corner in fear (1 Kings 21:20), and turn a whole nation back to God by calling fire down from heaven (1 Kings 18:36). James 5:17–18 describes him

> as a man subject to like passions as we are, and he prayed earnestly that it might not rain and it rained not on the earth by the space of three years and six months. And he prayed again, and the heaven gave rain, and the earth brought forth her fruit.

The secret to the accomplishments of Elijah was his fervency. James 5:16, in describing his modality of prayer, says, "The effectual fervent prayer of a righteous man avails much." As long as Elijah stayed fervent, his prayers were fast and furious in accomplishment. The Devil, however, prematurely ended Elijah's ministry by bedeviling him with the spirit of shame.

In 1 Kings 19:3–4, after greatly assaulting hell by killing the prophets of Baal, Jezebel threatened Elijah, and he said, "It is enough; now, O LORD, take away my life; for I am not better than my fathers."

When God appeared to him by a still, small voice on the mountain while he was on the run from Jezebel, he "wrapped his face in his mantle, and went out, and stood in the entering in of the cave" (1 Kings 19:13).

Shame starts when fervency and an honest relationship with God are eroded, As 2 Corinthians 3:18 says, "We all, with open face beholding as in a glass the glory of the Lord, are changed into the same image from glory to glory, even as by the Spirit of the Lord."

In these last days, when the last-days church is a typology of the spirit of Elijah (Malachi 4:5), we must guard against the spirit of shame. It stopped Elijah by reminding him of his forgettable past and keeping him from God's presence. We must beware lest we repeat the formula that led to Elijah's premature exit—shame.

Lot's Lamentations

Lot lived ashamed of the gospel. He was "vexed with the filthy conversation of the wicked" (2 Peter 2:7) but never preached or practiced the gospel to the people of Sodom and Gomorrah. Jesus said in Matthew 11:23, "If the mighty works, which have been done in thee [Capernaum] had been done in Sodom it would have remained until this day."

Lot sat at the gate of Sodom (Genesis 19:1), where decisions were made, but he never preached God to the city's people. They were so astounded at his sudden reversal in moral conscience when the angelic visitors were about to be raped; they said, "This one fellow came in to sojourn, and he will needs be a judge" (Genesis 19:9a).

He was ashamed of the gospel and ended ashamed in life. His wife turned into a pillar of salt for contravening God's Word (Genesis 19:26), he conceived through incest with his daughters (Genesis 19:33–38), and his family genealogy of Moabites and Ammonites became a byword for shame in Israel for countless generations.

His financial wherewithal that made Abraham's and his men unable to inhabit the land (Genesis 13:5–6) soon petered out because he was ashamed of God. In Luke 17:32, the Bible asks us to "Remember Lot's wife." It is a reminder of the necessity of shameless obedience if we are to avoid shameful lives.

Adam's Albatross

Adam and Eve were "both naked, the man and his wife, and were not ashamed" (Genesis 2:25). They had been placed in the garden of Eden "to dress and keep it ... But of the tree of the knowledge of good and evil, thou shalt not eat of it" (Genesis 2:15, 17).

They had full dominion over all creatures and were shameless in their relationship with God. When the Devil came, however, he made them desire what they shouldn't, and "the eyes of them both were opened, and they knew that they were naked" (Genesis 3:7).

They went from glory to shame by sin. They lost their position of dominion in an instant and became ashamed. Genesis 3:8 says, "They heard the voice of the LORD God walking in the garden in the cool of the day and Adam and his wife hid themselves from the presence of the LORD God amongst the trees of the garden."

God had predestined them for glory, but one moment of disobedience to His word short circuited that glorious destiny. His will for believers, "whom he did foreknow [and] ... predestinate to be conformed to the image of his Son ... [is they be] called, justified and also glorified" (Romans 8:29–30).

To enter this glory, however, we must avoid Adam's albatross. We must eschew "all that is in the world, the lust of the flesh, and the lust of the eyes, and the pride of life [that] is not of the Father, but is of the world" (1 John 2:16).

Afghanistan Girl's Battle Against Shame

Aesha Mohammadzai was betrothed at age twelve to a Taliban warlord in Afghanistan as compensation for her father's debts. She had no say in the marriage and was treated as a commodity of barter.

Her to-be husband, who already had a multitude of wives, left her with his extended family for upkeep. While there, Aesha was physically and emotionally abused and was made to sleep in an animal shed.

One day, she mustered enough courage to run away, but she was caught by the Taliban, who readily returned her to her husband-to-be. In a fit of rage, he cut off her nose and ears and macheted her hands.

She was left for dead in the mountains of Afghanistan but miraculously found a way to her grandfather's house. He took her to an American medical facility in Afghanistan from where she was transferred to medical facilities in the United States.

Since her arrival in the United States in 2011, she has undergone multiple corrective surgeries and psychotherapy for her dilemmas of shame and stigmatization. She has overcome all these trauma and is today unashamed and full of confidence.

She tells other victims of shame and torture, especially women, "Be strong and never give up and don't lose hope." Her hope persisted through her hurt, and the shame of a spited face has been replaced with the grace of a new beginning.

Humility is not humiliation.

Chapter Twelve

Spirit of Conceit

When pride cometh, then cometh shame but with the lowly is wisdom.
—Proverbs 11:2

Conceit is the greatest deceit in the twenty-first-century church. Words such as *self-actualization*, *self-confidence*, and *self-esteem* make the body of Christ feel good in the world but make us ashamed in the eyes of Christ.

The only confidence Christians are expected to have is confidence in God. Apostle Paul said in Philippians 3:3 that we, as true believers, are those who "worship God in the spirit, rejoice in Christ Jesus, and have no confidence in the flesh."

We must follow the example of early pioneers of the faith, such as John the Baptist, who said, "He [Jesus] must increase but I must decrease" (John 3:30). The modern-day egotistic, self-adulating, and prideful believer has no future in eternity. His or her end is guaranteed to be one of shame, but if a believer humbles him or herself, "under the mighty hand of God, He will exalt her in due time" (1 Peter 5:6).

Without Walls

Proverbs 25:27–28 says, "It is not good to eat much honey: so for men to search their own glory is not glory. He that hath no rule over his own spirit is like a city that is broken down, and without walls."

In Bible day, a city without walls was deemed vulnerable and a shame. For example, Nehemiah saw the broken-down walls of Jerusalem, and in Nehemiah 2:17, called on the men of Israel to rise and "build up the wall of Jerusalem, that we be no more a reproach."

Many walls are broken down by pride and conceit. This leaves cities that should be set in glory, according to Matthew 5:14, ashamed and damaged by increased rubbish. Nehemiah 4:2 says the wall consisted of "stones from heaps of rubbish which were burned."

The spirit of conceit makes a Christian ashamed. It crushes instead of catapults and ruptures instead of raptures a believer. The wise man said in Proverbs 16:18 that "pride goes before destruction, and an haughty spirit before a fall."

Pride: The Birthplace of Shame

Pride stopped a prospective great king of Israel. His name was Saul of Benjamin, and Samuel told him in 1 Samuel 13:13 that he "had done foolishly [and] not kept the commandment of the Lord God, which He commanded him. For now would the Lord have established his kingdom upon Israel for ever."

God wanted perfect obedience and would have perpetuated a dynasty of kings through Saul, but pride corrupted him and robbed him of God's glory. Samuel told him, "When thou was little in thine own sight, was thou not made the head of the tribes of Israel, and the Lord anointed thee king over Israel?" (1 Samuel 15:17).

The spirit of conceit makes shame inevitable. It exalts self and establishes shame. Psalm 119:78 says, "Let the proud be ashamed for they dealt perversely with me without a cause."

Saul died in battle on the hills of Gilboa in utter ignominy and shame. His death was described in 2 Samuel 1:21 as "the shield of the mighty vilely cast away [and] the shield of Saul, as though he had not been anointed with oil."

What happened to Saul was a miscarriage of opportunity due to pride and selfishness. No matter how high you rise, pride will bring you down to reality. Hosea 4:7 says, "as they [the Israelites] were increased, so they sinned against me [and] therefore will I change their glory into shame."

The Spirit of Korah

The spirit of Korah is the spirit of pride and insubordination, the spirit of self-exaltation and irreverence to authority. In Numbers 16:9, Moses described this spirit as exemplified by Korah the Levite and two hundred other princes of Israel.

> Seemeth it but a small thing unto you, that the God of Israel hath separated you from the congregation of Israel, to bring you near to himself to do the service of the tabernacle of the Lord, and to stand before the congregation to minister unto them?

Korah and the other renegade leaders wanted more than serving tables and cleaning lavers. They wanted the priesthood even though God had not called them into it. Pride is putting self before the Spirit of God and rewards before righteousness.

The spirit of Korah is, unfortunately, still alive in the church today. Jude (1:11, 13) described these believers who "perish in the gainsaying [or pride] of Core [Korah] [and are] raging waves of the sea [that] foam out their own shame."

The judgment of Korah was the near annihilation of his pedigree and a lifetime of shame that traversed generations. Numbers 16:32 says, "The earth opened her mouth, and swallowed [Korah] and their houses and all the men that appertained unto Korah and all their goods."

Attaining, Maintaining, and Retaining Glory by Humility

Pride means resisting God, and no one has ever won that contest. In 1 Peter 5:5, we learn, "Likewise, ye younger, submit yourselves unto the elder. Yea, all of you be subject one to another, and be clothed with humility: for God resisteth the proud, and giveth grace to the humble."

God gives grace to the humble, and this grace in turn births incontrovertible glory in a believer. Peter said he was a "partaker of the glory that shall be revealed" (1 Peter 5:1b).

Jesus came with a singular mission: "It became him, for whom are all things, and by whom are all things, [to] bring many sons unto glory" (Hebrews 2:10). He came so that "for our shame we can have double [glory]" (Isaiah 61:7) and walk in utter amazement to the hosts of heaven because "He has crowned us with glory and honor" (Psalm 8:5b).

When the "crown of pride [from] the drunkards of Ephraim be trodden under feet ... [God will] in that day be for a crown of glory and for a diadem of beauty unto the residue of his people" (Isaiah 28:3, 5).

When pride is eliminated, glory becomes inestimable and inevitable. It makes you shine like a shooting star and leave a lasting sparkle wherever you go. God wants to make our lives glorious, but keeping the glory by not staying humble is the greatest challenge many in the church face daily.

Pastor Shane's Story

As a young, irrepressible pastor, Shane Warren wanted to affect the lives of untold millions with the gospel. He became the pastor of a church in Tennessee and poured himself into it. The church had experienced no growth, and the community seemed to be difficult ground to possess. In three years, however, Pastor Warren saw his congregation multiply exponentially. He had reached a record 150 members and was ecstatic.

One day while praying, he told God, "We did it!" to which God replied, "Who is we?" Unaware of the spite his self-adulation and personal egotism had meant to God, he was soon faced with his lack of humility. He was falsely accused of some internal shenanigans at his church and was relieved of his pastoral responsibilities for three years. He spiraled into a state of depression and in a state of frenzy came close to killing himself several times.

While he was in this state, God reminded him of his prayer, "We did it!" He instantly repented, and within thirty days, he was restored to a pastorate bigger and more glorious than his former one.

He had become ashamed because of his fullness of self and emptiness of his spirit. God restored the favor over him as a result of his humility and obedience to God's Word. Proverbs 13:18 says, "Poverty and shame shall be to him that refuses instruction: but he that regards reproof shall be honored."

When you know the secrets, you cannot remain a secret.

Chapter Thirteen

Spirit of Covering

For it is a shame even to speak of those things which are done of
them in secret. But all things that are reproved are made manifest
by the light for whatsoever doth make manifest is light.
—Ephesians 5:12–13

Your greatest attainments in life will be at the place of discovery. Benjamin Franklin said, "If you think education is expensive, try ignorance." Ignorance will cost you your glory and embolden your shame.

The psalmist said in Psalm 34:5, "They looked unto him and were lightened and their faces were not ashamed." When you look on His Word, you get light, and light abrogates shame.

Too many Christians look inside or around them for answers to life's questions. The answer is not around or within but above. Hebrews 12:1–2 tells those who are "compassed about with so great a cloud of witnesses [to] lay aside every weight, and the sin which doth so easily beset us, and run with patience the race [by] looking unto Jesus the author and finisher of our faith."

Don't Cover—Just Discover

When you make discovery a core aspect of your spiritual life, you make glory and honor inevitable. Proverbs 25:2 says, "It is the glory of God to conceal a thing: but the honor of kings is to search out a matter."

Job became the greatest man in the east on the platform of discovery. He refused to be content with superficial, fluffy, business-as-usual Christianity, and by so doing, he bequeathed a legacy of glory to his ancestors.

In Job 29:3–4, Job said, "His [God's] candle shined upon my head, and by His light I walked through darkness when the secret of God was upon my tabernacle." The rigors of shame are birthed in the dark pangs of ignorance of God's Word.

Proverbs 3:35 says, "The wise shall inherit glory but shame shall be the promotion of fools." Until you invite the light of God's Word into your circumstance and uncover to discover, you will continually grope in the dark, ashamed.

Study Never to Be Ashamed

Anyone can walk with a head held high and live a shameless life if he or she studies the Bible. It is not enough just to read the Bible; we must do a comprehensive, in-depth study to unravel the hidden mysteries of God's Word. "Study to shew thyself approved unto God, a workman that needeth not to be ashamed, rightly dividing the word of truth" (2 Timothy 2:15).

Shame is simply a choice not to study. Rather than study the Word of God, many Christians seek quick fixes that have no roots. They live fast but lose life because they follow the shallow principles of the world and not the substance of God's Word. The psalmist described them as wallowing in shame because of their lack of desire for God's Word. In Psalm 119:80, David prayed, "Let my heart be sound in thy statutes that I be not ashamed."

The Anointing for Shameless Living

Until you are anointed, your shame is nonnegotiable. "Wine makes glad the heart of man, oil make[s] his face to shine and bread strengthens man's heart" (Psalm 104:15). The wise man added in Ecclesiastes 8:1b, "A man's wisdom makes his face to shine, and the boldness of his face shall be changed."

The secret to a shameless, shining life is wisdom taught by the anointing of the Holy Spirit.

> The anointing which ye have received of him abideth in
> you, and ye need not that any man teach you: but as the
> same anointing teacheth you of all things, and is truth, and
> is no lie, and even as it hath taught you, ye shall abide in
> him. And now, little children, abide in him; that, when he
> shall appear, we may have confidence, and not be ashamed
> before him at his coming. (1 John 2:27–28)

When you are taught of the Holy Spirit's anointing, according to Ecclesiastes 8:1 and 1 John 2:28, you walk in boldness, not in shame. The reason why so many believers are ashamed at the altar is because they have replaced the anointing that teaches within with the religious rudiments and traditions of today. Jesus said that you "have made the commandment of God of none effect by your tradition" (Matthew 15:6). Until you get off the saddle of tradition and fly on the wings of the eagle far above every human understanding, you will never taste true glory and forfeit shame. Exodus 19:4–5 says,

> Ye have seen what I did unto the Egyptians, and how I bare
> you on eagles' wings, and brought you unto myself. Now
> therefore, if ye will obey my voice indeed, and keep my
> covenant, then ye shall be a peculiar treasure unto me
> above all people: for all the earth is mine.

Discovery: The Birthplace Of Recovery

Rev. Ashbrook, the then-Louisiana state district overseer for the Assemblies of God, had just been told by a surgeon that he had less than six months to live. He had an inoperable lung mass, and even the best of treatment would prolong his life for only a year.

In that one moment, the revered gentleman and his wife faced down the bewildered surgeon and told him that in the absence of a cure from medicine or surgery, they would depend on God for his healing.

That was in 1958. Rev. Ashbrook lived another fifty years and pastored megachurches in Hong Kong, Albania, and West Monroe, Louisiana. Even though his faith was severely challenged on several occasions, he never quit.

Rev. Ashbrook's healing secret was the discovery of a pivotal Scripture that changed his life and his health. He found out that "if the Spirit of him that raised up Jesus from the dead dwell in you, he that raised up Christ from the dead shall also quicken your mortal bodies by his Spirit that dwelleth in you" (Romans 8:11).

He realized that the Holy Spirit in him could do what he needed—quicken his mortal body. He lifted up his arms in surrender while at the meeting and went from coughing up bloody sputum on the pulpit to living another fifty years in near-perfect health. As a testimony to the quickening power of the Holy Spirit, he preached three services every Sunday in his seventies, and at the time of his passing at nearly age ninety, he was actively involved in ministry and missions.

Killing time is not murder—it's suicide.

Chapter Fourteen

Spirit of Confusion

A wise servant shall have rule over a son that causeth shame, and
shall have part of the inheritance among the brethren.
—Proverbs 17:2

The true test of a mandate or vision from God is sustainability. Gamaliel, the wise lawyer in the days of the early church, said, "If it be of God, ye cannot overthrow it; lest haply ye be found even to fight against God" (Acts 5:39).

Many glorious destinies have been overthrown not by lack of vision but by duplication or replication of visions. Jesus said, "One thing is needful and Mary hath chosen that good part, which shall not be taken away from her" (Luke 10:42).

The single eye is the precursor for the glorious, light-filled body. Luke 11:34 says, "When thine eye is single, thy whole body also is full of light." Shame has bestridden our generation as a colossus because we lack vision and instead walk in confusion.

The glorious, last-day army that will herald Jesus' return is described in Joel 2:7 as they who "run like mighty men [and] climb the wall like men of war and [who] march every one on his ways and do not break their ranks." Our strength as a church lies in our focusing, fighting, and finishing strong. If we become confused, on the other hand, we will falter, fail, and end up ashamed.

Noah's Nebulousness

Noah had lived an exemplary life. He had preached the same message for a hundred years, built the largest boat of his day without ever seeing water from the sky, and led his wife and the families of his children to safety while the rest of the world was destroyed.

In one moment of confusion, however, his legacy turned from glory to shame. He cursed his youngest son, Ham, for exposing his nakedness while drunk, and that curse still stands today. Genesis 9:21–22, 25 says that Noah

> drank wine, and was drunken and was uncovered within his tent … And Ham, the father of Canaan, saw the nakedness of his father, and told his two brethren without … and Noah said, Cursed be Canaan; a servant of servants shall he be unto his brethren.

A man who commanded God's attention, wherefore God made a covenant with him (Genesis 9:15–17), became a progenitor of the Canaanites, who lived in idolatry and shame because of one moment of nebulousness.

Nebulous means "hazy" or "indistinct." Noah, while under the influence of alcohol, exposed himself to those passing by and brought a curse on Canaan as a result. His lack of perception or confusion started a lifetime of shame for the Canaanites that persists till this day.

Present-day Canaanites include inhabitants of Israel, Jordan, Syria, and Lebanon and include those with Ammonite, Moabite, Israelite, and Phoenician heritage. These are, because of Noah's nebulousness, still servants of Shem and Japheth (Genesis 9:25–27).

The Cain Code

Cain lived the life of a vagabond, a wanderer or confused individual. He killed his brother, Abel, and as a result, God cursed him.

> Thou cursed from the earth, which hath opened her mouth to receive thy brother's blood from thy hand; When thou tillest the ground, it shall not henceforth yield unto thee

her strength; a fugitive and a vagabond shalt thou be in the earth. (Genesis 4:11–12)

Cain had a life so full of confusion and shame that he said, "I shall be a fugitive and a vagabond in the earth; and it shall come to pass, that every one that findeth me shall slay me" (Genesis 4:14b).

The Cain code destroys glorious destinies by making people vagabonds. They shine but only for a moment, and they end up in ignominy and shame as a result of indecision.

Believers are warned about the nemesis of the Cain code; Jude 1:11, 13 says,

Woe unto them! for they have gone in the way of Cain ... [and are] raging waves of the sea, foaming out their own shame [and] wandering stars, to whom is reserved the blackness of darkness for ever.

If you want to enter a life of sustainable glory, stop wandering and start walking in divine wisdom. James 3:17 says, "The wisdom that is from above is first pure, then peaceable, gentle, and easy to be intreated, full of mercy and good fruits, without partiality, and without hypocrisy."

Your Glory Is Due to His Guidance

The tapestry of glory is incomplete without divine guidance. Isaiah 58:8b says, "The glory of the LORD shall be thy reward" because "the LORD shall guide thee continually, and satisfy thy soul in drought" (Isaiah 58:11a).

Confusion annihilates glory by halting instead of hastening the way God wants us to take. In Zephaniah 3:19, God said, "I will undo all that afflict thee and save her that halteth, and gather her that was driven out and I will get them praise and fame in every land where they have been put to shame."

God promises to turn your shame into fame when you stop halting and start heeding divine guidance. As long as Israel hindered, hesitated, or halted the move of God, it remained ashamed. When God guided its people, however, their renown and praise went forth.

The Last Day's Glorious Army

God's last-day soldiers are characterized by vision. They run their race, follow the Lord, and remain resolute to the end. Joel 2:8b says, "They shall walk every one in his path and when they fall upon the sword, they shall not be wounded."

Issachar was considered the leader among His brethren not because of his might or military wherewithal but because they "were men that had understanding of the times, to know what Israel ought to do [and] the heads of them were two hundred and their brethren were at their commandment" (1 Chronicles 12:32).

Divine direction is the inevitable path to destiny distinction. When it is absent, shame is unalterable. Psalm 109:29 says, "Let mine adversaries be clothed with shame, and let them cover themselves with their own confusion, as with a mantle."

Wherever confusion is present, shame is not far behind. But wherever the Spirit of God guides, glory is attained. Isaiah 28:5–6 says, "In that day shall the LORD of hosts be for a crown of glory and for a diadem of beauty, unto the residue of his people and for a spirit of judgment to him that sitteth in judgment."

Glory from Gimbie

I arrived in New York after having worked as a missionary doctor in Gimbie, Ethiopia, for three months. I was given no chance at employment in the American health care system as a physician, so my family and peers advised me to return to my London base.

Even though I had passed all my entry-level exams, I had average scores and had no connections with anyone in the residency program. My friends and family called me overambitious, adventurous, stubborn, and proud, and they asked me to return to London to start my career, but I knew God's voice!

He had sent me to New York and had reassured me He would complete the call by finding me a job. Within a month and a half of arriving in New York, I was offered a surgical residency position, and I became an attending consultant in the American medical system.

Eight years later, I have risen to the top of my chosen field as a fellow of the American Academy of Family Physicians. I am the medical director of a thriving practice and on the board of directors of the state academy of family physicians.

I had followed God to Ethiopia, and He had shown up for me in New York. There is glory wherever God guides, and His supply and sustainability follows you wherever He sends you.

Until you learn to be silent before God, you will be silenced by men.

Chapter Fifteen

Spirit of Clamor

A foolish woman is clamorous: she is simple, and knoweth nothing.
—Proverbs 9:13

Believers need to reawaken the lost devotion of waiting on the Lord in their quiet time. The average Christian spends less than a minute daily in prayer, while the average pastor spends about thirty minutes daily in prayer. Isaiah 40:31 says,

> The youth shall faint and be weary, and the young men shall utterly fall but they that wait upon the LORD shall renew their strength; they shall mount up with wings as eagles; they shall run, and not be weary; and they shall walk, and not faint.

The eagle is not a bird that is easily ashamed. It is famed for its foliage and its eyesight, which is sixteen times more precise than a human's. It is the symbol of the greatest nation on earth, the United States, and has represented valiant Christianity for thousands of years.

All these, however, would remain elusive if the eagle were clamorous. To be clamorous means to shout vehemently or insistently with a loud, persistent cry. An eagle does not run with the crowd scavenging for dead flesh but rather, in isolation and keen perception hunts for prey. Isaiah 64:4 says, "Since the beginning of the world men have not heard, nor perceived by the ear, neither hath the eye seen ... what [God] hath prepared for him that waits for him" (Isaiah 64:4).

Empty Drums Make the Most Noise

The noisiest people are the most clamorous. They are, according to Proverbs 9:13, loud, boisterous, and empty individuals who want to talk more than listen. The world is waiting for stable and still lovers of God's Word. It is tired of the loud, abrasive, and empty Christian who remains worldly and weighed down by life. This sort is described in 2 Timothy 3:2 as "lovers of their own selves, covetous, boasters, proud, blasphemers, disobedient to parents, unthankful [and] unholy." Their end will be shameful, according to 2 Timothy 3:8–9, because they are "corrupt minds, reprobate concerning the faith [and] shall proceed no further for their folly shall be made manifest unto all men as theirs also was."

Until you learn to be silent before God, you will be silenced by men. They will leave you beleaguered and burdened with life's assaults instead of being blessed by being still before Him. Psalm 46:10 says, "Be still, and know that I am God."

The Secret Place

Many want it without waiting on God for it. Psalm 91:1 says, "He that dwells in the secret place of the most High shall abide under the shadow of the Almighty."

If the church must abide in God's shadow, it must first enter and dwell in His secret place. When you dwell in His secret place, God Himself becomes your refuge, and shame cannot come near you (Psalm 91:9–10).

Even Jesus in his earthly sojourn had a secret place. Before He chose the twelve disciples, He prayed all night (Luke 6:12). He made solitary prayer such a common custom (Mark 1:35) that the disciples asked Him to teach them to pray likewise (Luke 11:1).

A servant is not greater than his master, and if Jesus needed a secret place, so do we. Prayer is not a luxury but a necessity to survive the brutality of these last days and its attendant causalities. Psalm

25:3 says, "Let none that wait on thee be ashamed," and Isaiah 49:23b testifies, "They shall not be ashamed that wait for me."

Attention = Attitude + Tension

Jude 1:12-13 describes the clamorous Christian as "clouds without water, carried about of winds; trees whose fruit wither, without fruit, twice dead, plucked up by the roots [and] raging waves of the sea, foaming out their own shame." The paradox is that these, who are twice dead, are the same ones raging and foaming out their shame.

What will catapult or cripple believers in the modern church is their stillness or instability in God's presence respectively. Saul would have made his dynasty a lineage of kings if he had paid less attention to the boisterousness of his men and more attention to God's business on the altar (1 Samuel 13:11–12). Because he refused to wait on the Lord, Saul missed his *kairos* moment of destiny; he had listened to men instead of God. Instead of a legacy of glory, he left a legacy of shame for his family.

When men start attending to God's Word, the glorious church will again be manifested and be heralded around the world. Proverbs 4:25–26 says, "Let thine eyes look right on, and let thine eyelids look straight before thee. Ponder the path of thy feet, and let all thy ways be established."

Diabetic Foot Ulcer

In my final medical school exams, I needed to pass medicine and surgery to become a medical doctor. While my colleagues were burning the midnight oil, I spent adequate time studying but never compromised with my church or prayer time.

On the morning of the most important exam of my career, I spent about one hour praying to God about the day. I got into my car and, as I was about to drive off, I noticed a scrawly written note: "Diabetic Foot Ulcer" on my dashboard.

In utter amazement, I checked my car windows and doors and noted they were sealed. This flimsy note hadn't been on my dashboard the night before, and as I was about to throw it away, the Holy Spirit spoke to me. He told me the exam question would be on diabetic foot ulcer and advised me to review that condition. This instruction puzzled me because in the thirty-year history of our medical school, a question on diabetic foot ulcer had never been asked.

I, however, knew His voice, and I studied diabetic foot ulcer in depth. Out of the six essay questions asked in the exam, diabetic foot ulcer was one. I passed the exam with flying colors and graduated gloriously at the top of my class.

I passed those final exams not because of my intelligence but because of my secret place in the Lord. I shattered academic and spiritual records in my journey through medical school because I had listened and learned from Him and not because I had labored more than my peers had.

Until you are full time (for God), you cannot carry full fire (to the world).

Chapter Sixteen

Spirit of Coldness

And because iniquity shall abound, the love of many shall wax cold.
—Matthew 24:12

The spirit of coldness is an antichrist spirit that starts with a lack of zeal for God's work and ends up in shame. In Revelation 3:15–16, Jesus said, "I know thy works, that thou art neither cold nor hot: I would thou wert cold or hot. So then because thou art lukewarm, and neither cold nor hot, I will spue thee out of my mouth."

Until there is a fire burning within, shame is inevitable. The fire of the Holy Spirit in the believer is an antidote to shame and the spirit of coldness its guarantee. God chose to spew out the lukewarm (Revelation 3:15) than tolerate them, because even God abhors the spirit of coldness. Jeremiah 20:9, 11 says,

> His word was in mine heart as a burning fire shut up in my bones, and I was weary with forbearing, and I could not stay ... But the Lord is with me as a mighty terrible one: therefore my persecutors shall stumble, and they shall not prevail: they shall be greatly ashamed; for they shall not prosper.

The church is guaranteed shameless living and its enemies shameful existence when its members carry the fire of God in their bones. What can be fired can't have died!

Evangelism: Our Supreme Task

Only those who multiply themselves by outreach can turn away the enemies at the gate and so not be ashamed. Isaiah 28:5–6 says,

> In that day shall the Lord of hosts be for a crown of glory, and for a diadem of beauty, unto the residue of his people, and for a spirit of judgment to him that sitteth in judgment, and for strength to them that turn the battle to the gate.

Psalm 127:4–5 says,

> As arrows are in the hand of a mighty man; so are children of the youth. Happy is the man that hath his quiver full of them: they shall not be ashamed, but they shall speak with the enemies in the gate.

Our lack of communication of what we believe is the reason for our shame. The apathy and reclusiveness of so-called Christians in sharing their faith is the paramount reason for shame at his second coming. We read in 1 John 2:28, "And now, little children, abide in him; that, when he shall appear, we may have confidence, and not be ashamed before him at his coming."

The only reason God kept us on earth after our salvation was to preach the gospel and by so doing to win the lost. Psalm 11:46 says, "I will speak of thy testimonies also before kings, and will not be ashamed," and Daniel 12:3b says, "They that turn many to righteousness [shall shine] as the stars for ever."

Five Foolish Virgins

Jesus' parable about the five foolish and seven wise virgins is centered on how shame can be stopped by lack of fire or started by its presence. In Matthew 5:8, the "foolish said unto the wise, give us of your oil; for our lamps are gone out." If you want to carry the glory and power of God and not be ashamed at His return, always carry the fire of the Holy Spirit. The five foolish virgins lost their fire, were rejected at the marriage supper of the Lamb (Matthew 25:11–12), and ended their journey in shame.

It was not the lack of virginity that hindered the five foolish virgins from entering the marriage feast of the Lamb; it was their coldness or lack of fire. When they attempted to enter the feast, the bridegroom said, "Verily I say unto you, I know you not" (Matthew 25:12b).

Their greatest experience was robbed from them by a lack of Holy Spirit fire in their time of need. They laid their wicks in the spirit of coldness and at their time of need ended up ashamed at the altar.

Live and Love Unashamed

If believers have fervent love among them (1 Peter 4:8), they will never be ashamed another day of their lives. Love that is fervent is more than just passionate. It is full of fire and causes "hope not [to be] ashamed because the love of God is shed abroad in our hearts by the Holy Ghost which is given unto us" (Romans 5:5).

Only those who stop fervent love from flowing through them to others end up ashamed; 1 John 4;17 says, "herein is our love made perfect, that we may have boldness in the day of judgment."

Love is like a pipeline that always ends up in glory rather than shame. It spurs boldness, not browbeaten intimidation or insecurity. As long as we love only those who love us and hate those who hate us, we remain as they are—ashamed at the altar. We must forgive and live in love for the glory of God to reside in us. We read in 1 Peter 4:16, "If any man suffer as a Christian, let him not be ashamed; but let him glorify God on this behalf."

Pastor Who Died in Onitsha

Pastor Daniel Ekechukwu is the pastor of Power Chapel in Onitsha, Nigeria. He crashed into a stone pillar in 2000 and suffered internal injuries and was unconscious for a day before he died. His wife, being a pastor's wife, thought of nothing but "women received their dead raised to life" (Hebrews 11:35). Instead of embalming him and preparing for the funeral, Pastor Ekechukwu's wife took the corpse from the mortuary to a church where Reinhard Bonnke was holding a meeting.

Evangelist Bonnke was leading a Fire Conference for three days, and some 37,000 pastors, evangelists, and church leaders were attending. They had an encounter with fire to bring unity to the body of Christ.

Pastor Ekechukwu had not breathed for three days and had been certified dead by a medical professional. The cause of death was severe brain damage, and his corpse was placed in the basement of the megachurch.

Pastor Ekechukwu had been taken to the gates of hell as a result of his vindictive and unforgiving spirit toward his wife. As he was about to be ushered into hell, he heard *Reinhard Bonnke's voice calling him back to life. God told him to return to earth and warn the people about the dangers of unforgiveness and holding onto past hurts.

In the church, Pastor Ekechukwu's corpse drew a deep breath, and he came back to his faculties. He became known as the resurrection man and was reunited with his wife and family three days after he had been certified dead.

Today, he goes around the country testifying of the power of God over death and doom. He also warns the church against being partisan, petty, and proud in these last days as Jesus' imminent return beckons.

The ways of God are the highways of success.

Chapter Seventeen

Spirit of Contrariness

Sound speech, that cannot be condemned; that he that is of the contrary
part may be ashamed, having no evil thing to say of you.
—Titus 2:8

There is a contrary spirit sweeping through nations today. A spirit of revolt and rebellion coupled with a spirit of antagonism and animosity toward God has arisen and has caused billions worldwide to be ashamed. The end of such people, according to 2 Timothy 3:9, is folly, and folly begets shame. Proverbs 3:35 says, "The wise shall inherit glory: but shame shall be the promotion of fools."

We live in a generation of contrariness. The right is now called wrong and the wrong right. The spirit of contrariness is why, compared to previous generations, we have an upsurge in suicides, sickness, and scandals in the church. This upsurge is because this generation, though "professing themselves to be wise [have] become fools and changed the glory of the incorruptible God into an image made like to corruptible man" (Romans 1:22–23).

Wickedness Begets Unwellness

The ruin of this generation is an ancient albatross called sin. Just as it destroyed Samson and David, so it destroys lives today. Jeremiah 17:13 says, "Lord, the hope of Israel, all that forsake thee shall be ashamed."

You cannot live in wickedness and expect to walk in wellness all the days of your life. Who you oppose in life will determine your position in life. Proverbs 13:5b says, "A wicked man is loathsome, and cometh to shame."

Eli's sons, Hophni and Phinehas, were called sons of Belial (1 Samuel 2:12) because of their contrariness to God's Word. They turned Eli's legacy of fame into shame by their crass materialism and whoremongering.

This generation must replace its love of the world with a love for God and a hatred of evil if it is to see the glory of God again. Psalm 85:9 says, "His salvation is nigh them that fear him that glory may dwell in our land."

Bondage Bandit or Barrier Breaker

In Hebrews 6:6, believers who live contrary to the Word of God are described as "crucifying to themselves the Son of God afresh, and putting him to an open shame."

The goal of contrary spirits is to bequeath a legacy of shame to generations unborn by their attitude. Jude 19 says these contrary ones who foam out their own shame in Jude 13 are "th ey who separate themselves, sensual, having not the Spirit." This last-day, contrary spirit thrives on isolation that births shame. Proverbs 29:15 says, "A child left to himself brings his mother to shame."

The walk of faith in the last days will be an across-the-grain, protocol- breaking anathema to societal and cultural norms because we "walk by faith and not by sight" (2 Corinthians 5:7).

We read in 1 Peter 4:16, "Having a good conscience; that, whereas they speak evil of you, as of evildoers, they may be ashamed that falsely accuse your good conversation in Christ."

Faith: Our Greatest Tool against Shame

You cannot be more contrary to God than when walking in faithlessness. Those who end up ashamed in life walked out on faith. Romans 10:11 and 9:33 say, "Whosoever believeth on him shall not be ashamed."

In the Psalms, God promises us a lifetime devoid of shame if we trust in Him. Psalm 25:20 says, "Let me not be ashamed for I put my trust in thee," and Psalm 31:1 adds, "In thee, O Lord, do I put my trust; let me never be ashamed."

The power of a life activated by faith is shameless living. Faith makes you walk in unusual confidence and assuredness when everyone else is crestfallen and diminished in their intensity for God. The power to come boldly and unashamed to the altar starts with faith in Son of God Jesus Christ and doing His word.

Faith is the game changer in the climes of shame that is sweeping our world today. Hebrews 10:22–23 says,

> Let us draw near with a true heart in full assurance of faith, having our hearts sprinkled from an evil conscience, and our bodies washed with pure water. Let us hold fast the profession of our faith without wavering.

Until we trust in God, we will never know the greatness and glory He wants to give us.

Love: The Final Frontier Against Shame

You cannot be more like God than when walking in love, and you cannot be more contrary to God than when walking in hatred, unforgiveness, and bitterness. When you make things happen for others, God will make things happen for you.

The love for God and others will create an expectancy of glory when Jesus returns. In 1 John 2:28, Elder John adjures us, "Abide in him; that, when he shall appear, we may have confidence, and not be ashamed before him at his coming."

The key to abiding in God is lovingly obeying Him. John 15:9-10 says, "As the Father hath loved me, so have I loved you [and] if ye keep my commandments, ye shall abide in my love even as I have kept my Father's commandments, and abide in his love." Love is the final frontier to staying unashamed.

Those who bristle at the thought of loving others will inevitably have shame-filled lives. Psalm 35:26 says, "Let them be ashamed and brought to confusion that rejoice at mine hurt. Let them be clothed with shame and dishonor that magnify themselves against me."

The wise man in Proverbs 19:26 described what happens when we go contrary to the law of love: "He that wasteth his father, and chaseth away his mother, is a son that causeth shame, and bringeth reproach."

The result of not loving God or man is shame. The end product of walking in love is incontrovertible divine glory. Jesus said in John 17:24b that He wanted people to be where He is "that they may behold my glory, which thou hast given me for thou loves me before the foundation of the world."

Revival in Enugu

The school was in an uproar. One of our undergraduates had been raped by an unknown assailant on campus, and the students were getting very restive. They wanted vengeance by all means and were willing to burn down or sacrifice the school's academic calendar to achieve their aim.

The Christians on campus, however, began to pray for revival. A gathering for the Christians on campus was called, and God's intervention was requested to stop the impending clash. Miraculously, the disquiet died down as the school agreed to aggressively pursue the rapist.

I was in my second year of medical school and passionately wanted a genuine move of God on campus. The Holy Spirit orchestrated a gathering of different church denominations and fellowships that showed me the influence the church could wield if we prayed and stayed together.

After an extended time of prayer and fasting, things began to change on the campus. First of all, the leadership of the students' union became filled with Bible-believing Christians. The church became the most influential body in the land and saw unprecedented growth in numbers and infrastructure.

By the time I left five years later, Christians were respected and rewarded with choice elected positions at all levels of student governance. The school policy that had accommodated vices such as liquor and idolatry then featured events such as the consecration of the school hostels and regular prayer walks and meetings.

This campus, the University of Nigeria Enugu Campus (UNEC), was known as the most professional campus south of the Sahara and consisted of medical, law, business, and paramedical faculties. It had always been seen as unfruitful ground for revival, but through hearts yielded to consecration, UNEC saw a revival.

Quit focusing on your misses and focus on His mark.

—Pastor Shane Warren, lead pastor,
the Assembly West Monroe, Louisiana

Chapter Eighteen

Spirit of Condemnation

*Fear not; for thou shalt not be ashamed: neither be thou confounded; for
thou shalt not be put to shame: for thou shalt forget the shame of thy youth,
and shalt not remember the reproach of thy widowhood any more.*
—Isaiah 54:4

Shame brings the spirit of condemnation speedily. This condemnation can be self-condemnation, God condemnation, or human condemnation. The world thrives on condemnation, calumny, and comparison. Many want to be like the Joneses, and in the pursuit of their false dreams, they fall into condemnation.

What this generation needs to do is accept God's Word at face value. It says believers are not condemned but commended. John 5:24 says, "He that heareth my word, and believeth on him that sent me, hath everlasting life, and shall not come into condemnation." Until unbelievers turn to become the Maker's original, and not a poor imitation of someone or something else, they will remain ashamed.

Not Better than My Fathers

The spirit of Elijah is the dominant spirit characterizing the last-days church. Malachi 4:5–6 says,

> Behold, I will send you Elijah the prophet before the coming
> of the great and dreadful day of the Lord and he shall turn

the heart of the fathers to the children, and the heart of the children to their fathers.

The Devil wants to stop the latter-day army of God with the same spirit of condemnation he used against Elijah in 1 Kings 19. After killing 450 prophets of Baal and calling down fire from heaven, Elijah ran when he heard Jezebel's threat to kill him (1 Kings 18).

God approached him when he was hiding in a cave and asked, "What doest thou here, Elijah?" (1 Kings 19:9b). He answered, "I have been very jealous for the Lord God of hosts: for the children of Israel have forsaken thy covenant, thrown down thine altars, and slain thy prophets with the sword; and I, even I only, am left (1 Kings 19:10)."

He looked at his past instead of focusing on his future. He had a father friction (1 Kings 19:4) and saw himself as worthless. This spirit of self-condemnation precipitated the end of Elijah's ministry because in 1 Kings 19:16, God told him to anoint "Elisha the son of Shaphat of Abelmeholah to be prophet in thy room."

The spirit of condemnation stopped the ministry of Elijah, and it can stop the last-day Elijah army if we let it into our hearts. Elijah felt ashamed in God's presence and, instead of attempting to have an open-faced experience, "wrapped his face in his mantle, and went out, and stood in the entering in of the cave (1 Kings 19:13).

Your glory is tied to God's face, and when you lose face with God, you become ashamed. In 2 Corinthians 3:18, we read, "We all, with open face beholding as in a glass the glory of the Lord, are changed into the same image from glory to glory, even as by the Spirit of the Lord."

Spirit of Correction, Not Condemnation

The spirit of isolation brings condemnation, and that spirit generates thoughts of suicide that eventually kill destinies and bring shame to lives. Anyone who stays aloof from instruction and encouragement will inevitably live a life of shame.

Proverbs 29:15 says, "The rod and reproof give wisdom: but a child left to himself bringeth his mother to shame." When children refuse the rod of correction, which is the Word of God, they stay ashamed.

The isolated lifestyle is a life that brings condemnation. Elijah stayed isolated, having abandoned his servant (1 Kings 19:2), and went on a forty-day journey alone. His lack of correction left him bereft of instruction and so kept him ashamed.

Power of Praise

Proverbs 28:12 says, "When righteous men do rejoice, there is great glory: but when the wicked rise, a man is hidden." The glory of God is preceded by praise and shame by the spirit of condemnation. When you want the glory and power of God, you must start praising and stop condemning.

Jeremiah 17:14 says, "Heal me, O Lord, and I shall be healed; save me, and I shall be saved: for thou art my praise." God is not a condemner but one who commends. Until we see God as an edifier and not an eliminator, as a builder and not a bully, and as a corrector and not a canceller of futures, we will continue to live in self-condemnation.

Instead of focusing on the limitless possibilities in God, many Christians live in self-pity with a woe-is-me mind-set. That mentality shortchanges their destinies and hamstrings their future benefits.

Before the glorious outpouring of the Spirit, God said we shall "eat in plenty, and be satisfied, and praise the name of the Lord your God, that hath dealt wondrously with you and my people shall never be ashamed" (Joel 2:26–27).

Praise or commendation heralds glory, but self-condemnation precedes shame. Before Jesus "appears in his glory ... [there will be a] people which shall be created [to] praise the Lord" (Psalm 102:16, 18). The altar of praise provokes glory, but the altar built on self-condemnation emanates shame.

Exposé Experience

Prior to becoming a Christian in high school, I had taken an exam to get into medical school. I was successful in the exams but did not go in that year because of a change in government policy. I eventually took another entry exam and passed with even better scores—this time as a Christian.

However, a spirit of condemnation was haunting me about my conduct in the previous year's entry exams. I had gotten an unsolicited sheet of paper from a senior colleague containing some of the questions to be asked and had used that to prepare for the exam. Up to that point, my family, classmates, and colleagues had alluded to my brilliance as the reason for my excellent scores, so I felt I had to set the record straight. I told my parents and siblings about what happened and how I had benefited from an exposé. This was coming two to three years after the date of occurrence, and most people I confessed to thought nothing of it. After all, I hadn't used that particular exam to obtain admission. To me, however, it was deliverance from a spirit of condemnation.

When I exposed everything hidden in my life to the light of God's Word, according to John 1:5 and Ephesians 5:13, darkness and despair disappeared. I broke the spirit of condemnation and shame by exposing my exposé to the Excellency of God's Word.

PART V

Countering the Last Days' Outpouring of Shame

*Discard your past,
define your present and you
will design your future.*

Chapter Nineteen

Shame and the End-Time Church

If any man suffer as a Christian, let him not be ashamed but let him glorify God on this behalf for the time is come that judgment must begin at the house of God and if it first begin at us, what shall the end be of them that obey not the gospel of God?
—1 Peter 4:16–17

The end of the age is a time of great contrast between the world and the church. While the church lives in the glory, the world lives in shame. Isaiah 60:1–2 says,

> Arise, shine for thy light is come, and the glory of the Lord is risen upon thee ... darkness shall cover the earth, and gross darkness the people but the Lord shall arise upon thee and his glory be seen upon thee.

The end-time church is a glorious church according to Ephesians 5:27. God wants "to present [to] himself a glorious church, not having spot, wrinkle or any such thing but that it should be holy and without blemish." The end time is supposed to be a distinctive time for the body of Christ, not a dilapidated state of being as we see today.

Shame is not supposed to cohabit with the end-time church. Due to a lack of knowledge, however, shame has been tolerated instead of terminated in the body of Christ. Glory should be our status quo, not an exception or intermittent occurrence in the last-days church. It is the custodian and habitation of God's glory on the earth, and until the world sees something in it that it doesn't have, it won't come to it.

Shame Versus Salvation

Today is the acceptable time of salvation according to Isaiah 61:2–3.

> Proclaim the acceptable year of the LORD, and the day of vengeance of our God to comfort all that mourn. To appoint unto them that mourn in Zion, to give unto them beauty for ashes, the oil of joy for mourning, the garment of praise for the spirit of heaviness that they might be called trees of righteousness, the planting of the LORD, that he might be glorified.

When the acceptable time of salvation comes, shame disappears. We read in 1 Peter 4:16–17 that we who are living in these last days should stay unashamed and glorify God in these last days. When judgment starts, shame will be the criterion to determine those who are or are not saved. It says there will be no salvation for those who refuse to glorify God but choose to live ashamed due to their affliction.

Restoring the Ark of David

The end-time church has a divine mandate to restore the tabernacle of David. Acts 15:16–17 says, "After this I [Jesus] will return and build again the tabernacle of David which is fallen down and I will build again the ruins thereof, and set it up. That the residue of men might seek after the Lord."

The ark of David was instituted in glory, and before the second coming of Jesus Christ, the Gentiles must see that glory—not shame—to seek after the Lord. What we show the world determines what they will seek after.

David prayed "to see God's power and glory as he had seen them in the sanctuary" (Psalm 63:2). The glory of the ark was reminiscent of what Solomon had witnessed at the dedication of the temple (2 Chronicles 7:1–2).

An impotent and ashamed church is a spiritual sedative to the last days' revival. Rather than herald the harvest, it hinders it. The glorious church, on the other hand, spurs His imminent return. God told Jesus, "Sit on my right hand, until I make thine enemies thy foot stool" (Hebrews 1:13).

The victorious church heralds the return of the King. It puts all of God's enemies under the church's feet, and then the Lord Jesus will stand up and return. God will not allow Jesus to stand up when the church is weak, limp, and infirmed. A church victimized and humiliated by the Enemy cannot welcome back the Master; only a victorious and overcoming church can do that.

Spiritual Outpouring and Last Days' Glory

Until the church rejects the toga of shame and adorns itself with glory, there will be no outpouring of the Spirit with signs, wonders, and deliverance. Shame has put a limit on the spiritual encounters and experiences we as a generation have experienced.

Joel 2:29–30 says, "Upon the servants and upon the handmaids in those days will I pour out my spirit. And I will show wonders in the heavens and in the earth, blood, and fire, and pillars of smoke." Until the wind of God's Spirit breathes upon the church, wonders will be nonexistent.

The God who talked to Moses face-to-face and thundered on Mount Sinai wants to encounter this generation of believers in a greater way, but it must first remove the garment of shame, disgrace, and regret. In 2 Corinthians 3:16, 18, we learn,

> When [we] turn to the Lord, the veil shall be taken away ... but we all, with open face beholding as in a glass the glory of the Lord, are changed into the same image from glory to glory, even as by the Spirit of the Lord.

From Shameful Exit to Triumphant Return

Reinhard Bonnke left Nigeria in 1991 with a government decree banning him from ever returning. There were riots and arsonist attacks all over the city of Kano, where he and his team were organizing crusades, and the government stopped his crusades forthwith and asked him to leave and never return.

It was a retaliatory attempt by the northern oligarchy to stop the penetration of the gospel into Muslim-dominated northern Nigeria. The tempo of the ministry was reduced, as Nigeria was its major operations center, but nonetheless, Bonnke kept believing and trusting God to open doors for ministry in Nigeria.

Those doors opened in 1999 when a democratically elected federal government took over in Nigeria and rescinded earlier decrees, including those affecting Bonnke. In ten years, he organized mammoth crusades around the country that brought almost 70 million souls to the knowledge of Jesus.

He had left in shame but had returned in glory because the end of faith is always victory. In 1 John 5:4–5, we read,

> Whatsoever is born of God overcomes the world and this is the victory that overcomes the world, even our faith [and] who is he that overcomes the world, but he that believeth that Jesus is the Son of God?

Charisma can take you to the top, but only character will keep you there.

Chapter Twenty

Slaughtering Shame: The Fear of the Lord

Surely his salvation is nigh them that fear him; that glory may dwell in our land.
—Psalm 85:9

When you fear God, you automatically walk in the glory and power of God. The reason for the porosity of the glory in this generation is the lack of the fear of God. When people fear God, glory is inevitable and shame irreconcilable.

The man or woman who fears God will be marked out for excellence and exploits. Psalm 112:1–3 says,

> Blessed is the man that fears the LORD, that delights greatly in his commandments. His seed shall be mighty upon earth (and) the generation of the upright shall be blessed. Wealth and riches shall be in his house and his righteousness endures for ever.

Whoever fears God tastes the power and glory of God, but whoever denies God stays ashamed. Acts 10:35 says, "In every nation he that feareth him, and worketh righteousness, is accepted with him."

Abraham: From Abuse to Awe

Abraham sojourned in the land of Gerar, where the fear of God was nonexistent. In Genesis 20:11, Abraham said, "Surely the fear of God is not in this place and they will slay me for my wife's sake."

They took his wife, so God visited barrenness on the wives of the leaders of the city. Genesis 20:18 says, "the LORD fast closed up all the wombs of the house of Abimelech, because of Sarah Abraham's wife."

These same people who once vilified him and did not fear his God came to him in Genesis 21:22–23, saying,

> God is with thee in all that thou doest: Now, therefore swear unto me here by God that thou wilt not deal falsely with me, nor with my son, nor with my son's son: but according to the kindness that I have done unto thee, thou shalt do unto me, and to the land wherein thou hast sojourned.

This land that did not fear God and had shamed Abraham by taking away his properties (Genesis 21:25) and wife (Genesis 20:18) started fearing the God of Abraham because Abraham feared God and lived a God-fearing life.

In Genesis 22:12, God told Abraham, "I know that thou fears God, seeing thou hast not withheld thy son, thine only son from me." Abraham gave the people of Gerar evidence of the God they had not seen, and glory visited him.

In Genesis 24:1, we read, "Abraham was old, and well stricken in age: and the LORD had blessed Abraham in all things." What will take you from the shame of the world to the glory of God is the fear of God.

Joseph: From Jailbird to Judge

In Genesis 45:13, Joseph told his brothers to "tell my father of all my glory in Egypt, and of all that they had seen." He went from the prison to the palace, exchanging the shame of prison with the glory of Egypt, because he chose the fear of the Lord.

The secret to his rapid transformation was his fear of God. When tempted by Potiphar's wife, he fled and said, "How then can I do this great wickedness, and sin against God?" (Genesis 39:9). He chose her scorn and evil accusations above his personal security and went to jail because he feared God.

He ruled Egypt with probity and transparency and forgave all those who had offended him, choosing rather to defend them. Genesis 50:19–20 says, "Joseph Said Unto Them, Fear Not: For Am I In The Place Of God? But As For You, Ye thought evil against me; but God meant it unto good, to bring to pass, as it is this day, to save much people alive."

His glory manifested itself because he gave up his guarantees to security, such as personal wealth and recriminations, and chose to follow God's will for his life. Rather than fear man, he feared God, and God rewarded him with the glory only God can give.

God's Glory or Earth's Example

When believers fear God, they cannot be hidden. Psalm 60:4 says, "Thou hast given a banner to them that fear thee, that it may be displayed because of the truth." You become God's glory banner when you fear Him.

Matthew 5:16 says, "Let your light so shine before men, that they may see your good works, and glorify your Father which is in heaven." The life that reflects the glory of God must first fear God.

Malachi 4:2 says, "Unto you that fear my name shall the Sun of righteousness arise with healing in his wings; and ye shall go forth, and grow up as calves of the stall." Every believer has a choice: live in fear of humanity and be an earthly example of nothing eternal, or fear God and display God's glory to all who want to see it.

My Dad's Story

General Momah, my dad, was highly respected by his peers in the Nigerian army because of his principled stand and unusual integrity. My dad invited me to spend the night with him when he was attending a conference near my medical school.

On arrival at the guest house where my father was staying, I was shocked. Thinly clad females from my university were sitting in an expansive living room, waiting to be picked by the generalissimos and escorted to private rooms. Unabashedly, these young girls made advances at me, and even though I knew several of them from medical school, they pursued me with ferocious lust and lasciviousness.

My dad, meanwhile, was in his room waiting for me. When I asked him what the horde of girls was doing downstairs, he unassumingly answered that they had been invited by his colleagues and that he had had no part in it.

His integrity and uprightness preserved him. Psalm 25:21 says, "Let integrity and uprightness preserve me; for I wait on thee." While many of his colleagues died from HIV/AIDS or retired unceremoniously, he survived the shenanigans of the Nigerian army.

He rose to the top of his profession as a general and served the Federal Republic of Nigeria as its longest-serving minister of science and technology. He is now in his early seventies and has just released his most recent book, *Nigeria: Beyond Divorce* to a captivated country.

The Lord will not appear in His glory till He appears in His church gloriously.

Chapter Twenty-One

Slaughtering Shame: The Faith of the Lord

For the which cause I also suffer these things: nevertheless I am not ashamed: for I know whom I have believed, and am persuaded that he is able to keep that which I have committed unto him against that day.
—2 Timothy 1:12

The faith of God is available to every believer and is a surety out of shame. Paul asserts that he cannot be ashamed because he knows whom he believes in and who he is persuaded by—God. Stand fast and sure in God's Word, and glory will be your status quo wherever you go. As 1 Corinthians 2:5-7 says,

> Your faith should not stand in the wisdom of men, but in the power of God. Howbeit we speak wisdom among them that are perfect ... [by] speaking the wisdom of God in a mystery, even the hidden wisdom, which God ordained before the world unto our glory.

What you hold fast to is what will last in your life. What you question, however, is what will quit working in your life. Your faith level determines your glory level. As 2 Thessalonians 1:11-12 says, "God would ... fulfill ... the work of faith with power that the name of our Lord Jesus Christ may be glorified in you and ye in him."

Until we build our faith by hearing the Word of God repeatedly, we can't abrogate shame in the church. The psalmist prayed, "Let my heart be sound in thy statutes that I be not ashamed" (Psalm 119:80).

Faith in Jesus

Faith in Jesus is not on the exclusive list but on the essential list for believers. It is not a luxury good for a select few but an indispensable, everyday tool for anyone with a genuine heart who desires to serve the lost for Jesus' sake.

In Revelation 14:12, we read, "The patience of the saints ... are they that keep the commandments of God and the faith of Jesus." We are supposed to walk in the God kind of faith that "calls those things which be not as though they were" (Romans 4:17) and not just the ordinary faith of a believer if we are to escape shame.

God wants to move us from faith toward God to the faith of God if we are to change our world from shame to glory. Jesus told the disciples when He was faced with the dead fig tree in Mark 11:22–23 to

> have faith in God for whosoever shall say unto this mountain, be thou removed, and cast into the sea and shall not doubt in his heart, but shall believe that those things which he saith shall come to pass he shall have whatsoever he saith.

From Believing to Becoming

The church is called to go from believing to becoming. If we are to herald the glorious appearance of God on earth, we must have faith tried in the fire. As 1 Peter 1:7 advises, those in adversity and who currently undergo "the trial of their faith ... though it be tried with fire, might be found unto praise and honor and glory at the appearing of Jesus Christ."

Believing or faith in God is basic, entry-level Christianity. Hebrews 6:6 says, "Leave the principles of the doctrine of Christ [and] go unto perfection; not laying again the foundation of repentance from dead works, and of faith toward God."

Those who want to go from shame to glory, however, don't just believe as the devils do in James 2:19. They move their faith to the God level of faith and become what they believe. The church needs to become what it believes to bring Jesus back. Psalm 3:3 says the "Lord is a shield for me [and] my glory, and the lifter up of mine head."

Kingdom Commodity

When Jesus comes, he will not be looking for the *Financial Times* or to the stock markets or to currency exchange rates but for faith in the hearts of men (Luke 18:8). His only commodity for kingdom exchange from shame to glory will be faith.

In 1 John 2:28, Elder John advised "little children [to] abide in him that when he shall appear we may have confidence, and not be ashamed before him at his coming." Many will be ashamed on judgment day because their hearts were devoid of faith. We know the end of our faith is salvation (1 Peter 1:9), and the testing of our trust will determine our glory.

It is our trust in God that determines whether we triumph over our enemies. Psalm 31:1 says, "In thee, O Lord, do I put my trust; let me never be ashamed: deliver me in thy righteousness."

From Faith to Faith

My wife had successfully finished her master's degree in public health with flying colors. She had a perfect score and was accepted into the doctoral program in public health. She was, however, a foreign student and needed to pay in excess of tens of thousands of dollars to commence her program. We called other programs and asked for possible scholarships, but there was none available at that time.

Through it all, though, God persisted in reassuring my wife about a scholarship. My wife recalls a certain morning, after her morning devotion, when a voice spoke to her: "I will give you a scholarship." She was shocked because prior to that, she had questioned the ability of a believer to hear God's voice.

We kept saying, however, the miracle of scholarships would be made manifest. When all positions seemed to have been taken and there seemed to be no more hope, my wife met a professor who asked her to investigate what he called "the common market" scholarship. He said it was a proviso that allowed any resident of ten American states who were taking specific courses to have a fee waiver for the duration of the course. My wife applied, and 50 percent of her fees was slashed. On top of that, the remaining 50 percent was underwritten by her department. She applied and got a job as a graduate assistant in the department, and that paid the balance of her school fees. The scholarship challenge took my wife from faith to faith because God is a faithful God.

One moment of favor is worth a million years of labor.

Chapter Twenty-Two

Slaughtering Shame: The Favor of the Lord

In my favor have I had mercy on thee. Therefore thy gates shall be open continually; they shall not be shut day nor night; that men may bring unto thee the forces of the Gentiles, and that their kings may be brought ... the glory of Lebanon shall come unto thee.
—Isaiah 60:10–11,13

The favor of God obliterates shame and catapults a man or woman into glory. Psalm 102:13–15 says, "Thou shall arise, and have mercy upon Zion for the time to favor her, yea, the set time, is come ... So the heathen shall fear the name of the LORD, and all the kings of the earth thy glory."

Until the time for favor comes, glory cannot be manifested. It takes acceptance by God (favor) to gain approval of men (glory). Romans 14:18 says, "He that in these things serves Christ is acceptable to God, and approved of men."

Favor is more than an accessory to the Christian life. It is a major weapon for winning the war on shame. Psalm 30:5, 7 says God's "anger endures but a moment [and] in his favor is life ... [and] by His favor He has made my mountain to stand strong."

Favor is the life of God, and it is available to the righteous. Psalm 5:12 says God "will bless the righteous [and] with favor will He compass him as with a shield."

Glory Cloud Via Favor Currency

The past is irrelevant when it comes to favor. It requires only righteousness, and you can go from hated to helped, from forsaken to favored, and from goaded to glorified. Isaiah 60:15 says, "Whereas thou has been forsaken and hated, so that no man went through thee, I will make thee an eternal excellency [and] a joy of many generations."

It took one moment of favor to accomplish what a million years of labor would never have accomplished. Your glory does not depend on your labor but on God's favor. Psalm 44:3 says, "They got not the land in possession by their own sword, neither did their own arm save them: but thy right hand, and thine arm, and the light of thy countenance, because thou hadst a favor unto them."

Every victory Joshua and the armies of Israel tasted in the wilderness was because of divine favor, not human labor. If you work for everything you earn, you will not live very long. Favor makes for accelerated breakthroughs and deliverance. Exodus 12:36 says, "the Lord gave the people favor in the sight of the Egyptians, so that they lent unto them such things as they required. And they spoiled the Egyptians."

In one night, God turned around 430 years of shame by favor. They received enough wealth to sustain them, even unto building the tabernacle of David hundreds of years later.

Mary: The Evidence of Favor

When Mary, a seventeen-year-old virgin, was found with child in Luke 1 and was about to be put out, stoned, and shamed, an angel appeared to her and spoke favor over her. Luke 1:28–30 says,

> The angel came in unto her, and said, Hail, thou that art highly favored, the Lord is with thee: blessed art thou among women. And when she saw him, she was troubled at his saying, and cast in her mind what manner of salutation this should be. And the angel said unto her, Fear not, Mary: for thou hast found favor with God.

The mind-set of believers needs to change in respect to loving favor. Many are like Mary, troubled and unsure if they deserve it, but favor is not fair. If Mary had rejected the angel's salutation of favor and had lived in shame rather than favor, she would never have become the mother of Jesus. She accepted the toga of highly favored and gave birth to the One who still blesses humanity daily. Proverbs 22:1 says, "A good name is rather to be chosen than great riches, and loving favor rather than silver and gold."

Too many believers would rather live in shame than love favor. Deuteronomy 33:23 says, "Naphtali, satisfied with favor and full with the blessing of the Lord, possess thou the west and the south." When full of favor, the blessings are a sine qua non of a shameless life.

Joseph: The Apostle of Favor

Joseph was in Potiphar's house as a slave and was favored. Genesis 39:6 says Potiphar "left all that he had in Joseph's hand and he knew not ought he had, save the bread which he did eat. And Joseph was a goodly person, and well favored."

After been falsely accused by Potiphar's wife, he was cast into prison but again was favored by the prison authorities. Genesis 39:21 says, "the Lord was with Joseph, and shewed him mercy, and gave him favor in the sight of the keeper of the prison."

Joseph's feet were bound in chains (Psalm 105:18–20) but not his favor with God and man. Eventually, that favor took Joseph from the pit to the palace. Psalm 105:21–22 says Pharaoh "made him lord of his house, and ruler of all his substance to bind his princes at his pleasure and teach his senators wisdom."

As long as you have the favor of God, glory is inevitable. The architect of Joseph's glory was his favor with God and man. Joseph changed destinies of peoples and nations from poverty to prosperity, from scarcity to surplus, and from shame to glory by walking in favor. Favor is a game changer over shame.

Jesus Testimony or John's Tombstone

A critical difference between the ministry of Jesus and the life of John the Baptist was the absence of favor in the latter's life and ministry. Both were endued with the Spirit of God from birth (Luke 1:41), but John did not have favor.

In Luke 1:80, Luke the physician said John the Baptist "grew, and waxed strong in spirit, and was in the deserts till the day of his shewing unto Israel." Commenting about Jesus, however, in Luke 2:52, Luke said, "Jesus increased in wisdom and stature, and in favor with God and man."

The ministry of Christians can be full of shame or glory depending on whether they accept or reject the favor or acceptance of God. Ephesians 1:6 says, "You are accepted in the beloved" because of God's grace. Proverbs 16:15 says, "In the light of the king's countenance is life and his favor is as a cloud of the latter rain." Favor carries spiritual impact and changes your story from zero to hero. It builds spiritual momentum that can change a people.

Favor took Daniel from slave to three-time president across kingdoms and generations (Daniel 1:9). It also took a slave girl, Esther, from orphan to queen (Esther 2:15–17) in less than twenty-four hours.

Favor is the fastest route to going from shame to glory. It is capable of changing your destiny in the shortest amount of time.

Twenty-Four-Hour Miracle

I arrived New York after having worked as a missionary doctor in Gimbie, Ethiopia, but I was given no chance at employment in the American health care system as a physician. I had missed the critical "match" season during which most residents got signed up by hospitals and was doing an observership in a clinic.

My friends and family called my mission foolhardy and asked me to abandon ship. God, however, reassured me of his favor and ultimate goodwill in New York. Twenty-four hours later, I was holding a passport to prosperity.

I had never met or heard of Dr. Stephen Carryl. He was at the time the chair and program director of Brooklyn Hospital's general surgery program and was holding a clinic in the building in which I worked as a medical observer.

In the few minutes we interacted, I told him my goals for residency training, and twenty-fours later, I got a call asking me to see Dr. Carryl for immediate employment. That was the best news of my medical career!

I started work as a surgery resident within a few months and went on from there to rise to the top of my chosen field as a fellow of the American Board of Family Physicians and medical director in my office.

The result of going till the end is glory eternally.

Chapter Twenty-Three

Slaughtering Shame: The Finishing of the Lord

So Moses finished the work. Then a cloud covered the tent of the
congregation, and the glory of the Lord filled the tabernacle. And Moses
was not able to enter into the tent of the congregation, because the cloud
abode thereon, and the glory of the Lord filled the tabernacle.
—Exodus 40:33–35

Kingdom glory is the end result of a finished product. Too many have lost their glory to incomplete assignments and abandoned projects. The minute Moses finished the assignment of furnishing and building the tabernacle, the glory of God invaded the temple. Divine glory is seen only when an earthly work is completed. In John 17:4–5, Jesus prayed to the Father,

> I have glorified thee on the earth: I have finished the work which thou gavest me to do. And now, O Father, glorify thou me with thine own self with the glory which I had with thee before the world was.

Not everyone is eligible for the glory; it is the privilege of finishers and not the right of every Christian. Proverbs 13:19 says, "The desire accomplished is sweet to the soul but it is abomination to fools to depart from evil." Glory does not manifest itself at the point of obedience to the task but at the point of completion.

The Spirit of Glory

Jesus told the disciples, "Ye shall be hated of all men for my name's sake but he that endureth to the end shall be saved" (Matthew 10:22). Even if you need to go against the grain of public opinion or naysayers to do God's will, keep going till you complete the assignment. As 1 Peter 4:14 says, "If ye be reproached for the name of Christ, happy are ye; for the spirit of glory and of God resteth upon you." At the end of the assignment amidst adversity is the spirit of glory.

Paul reminds us in 2 Corinthians 4:16–17 that "our outward man perishes, yet the inward man is renewed day by day. For our light affliction, which is but for a moment, works for us a far more exceeding and eternal weight of glory."

Abandoned and Ashamed

In Luke 14:28–30, Jesus said,

> Which of you, intending to build a tower, sits not down first, and counts the cost, whether he have sufficient to finish it? Lest haply, after he hath laid the foundation, and is not able to finish it, all that behold it begin to mock him, saying, This man began to build, and was not able to finish.

You are not ashamed because you didn't start right but because you failed to finish. The grace to finish makes the glory of finishing evident to all, but abandoning it midstream causes you perpetual shame.

The glory of God is heaven's stamp of approval on a well-finished earthly product. When Paul finished his work on earth, he said, "I have fought a good fight, I have finished my course, I have kept the faith: Henceforth there is laid up for me a crown of righteousness" (2 Timothy 4:7–8).

Tomorrow's glory takers are today's assignment finishers. Life is not glorious incomplete, and fullness does not equate with finishing. The rich man in Luke 12:19 said,

I will say to my soul, Soul, thou hast much goods laid up for many years; take thine ease, eat, drink, and be merry" but God gave him an ultimatum saying "this night thy soul shall be required of thee: then whose shall those things be, which thou hast provided? (Luke 12:20)

The grace to finish will guarantee glory. Stop running on your own strength and start depending on the mighty hand of God.

God Is a Finisher

When Jesus came to earth, He was not content with just healing the sick and raising the dead alone because He knew that "to this end was He born, and for this cause came He into the world, that He should bear witness unto the truth" (John 18:37).

He became the cynosure of all eyes and the central theme for the ages because he finished his assignment. In John 4:34, He told His disciples, "My meat is to do the will of him that sent me, and to finish his work."

As God's express image on the earth, believers are made to be finishers, just like God. God has never abandoned a project midway, and He promises He who has "begun a good work in you will perform it until the day of Jesus Christ."

God is a finisher, and He will strengthen you till the end. Isaiah 42:4 says, "He shall not fail nor be discouraged, till he have set judgment in the earth." Not every journey finishes strong, and as a result, not every life ends in glory. Your glory is subject to the completion of your assignment. God does not give gifts to commencers but only to completers on the journey of life.

T. L. Osborne versus William Branham

T. L. and Daisy Osborne set out for India as missionaries in their late teens. They returned a year later, bamboozled by the mission; they had been unable to win any sizeable number of converts. They were devastated and forlorn and returned to a pastorate in Portland, Oregon.

A few years later, T. L. Osborne was at a revival meeting at which William Branham was ministering. The power of God was so real that the sick were healed, people's identities (including driver's license numbers and addresses), were revealed, and God was glorified.

The Lord spoke to T. L. Osborne in that meeting, saying, "You too can do this." He believed this, and he relaunched his ministry. He later had a vision of the Lord in which God didn't have any hands. God said, "You are my hands." From that day, till he died at age eight-nine on February 14, 2013, T. L. Osborne never stopped preaching the gospel. He planted more than 150,000 new churches and sponsored over 30,000 men and women as full-time missionaries to unevangelized tribes and villages.

He held crusades in over ninety countries in which the name of Jesus had not been mentioned, and he attracted up to 500,000 people to evangelistic campaigns characterized by practical healings of lepers, the lame, and the blind.

William Branham, on other hand, started seeing his evangelistic crusades flounder. He spoke about himself being the last-days Elijah and denied the existence of the Trinity. His biblical doctrines marginalized a lot of mainline denominations, and preachers uncomfortable with his "new" doctrine restricted his ministry in their churches.

He died on December 24, 1965, after an automobile accident in Texas. His legacy died after his death, and his worldwide ministry was limited to a radio, tape, and magazine ministry.

Without the Holy Spirit, Christianity is just posing and not potent.

Chapter Twenty-Four

Slaughtering Shame: The Fire of the Lord

Now when Solomon had made an end of praying, the fire came down from heaven, and consumed the burnt offering and the sacrifices and the glory of the LORD filled the house. And the priests could not enter into the house of the LORD, because the glory of the LORD had filled the LORD's house.
—2 Chronicles 7:1–2

Whenever the fire of God falls, the glory of God follows. The glory of God is symbolic of the presence of God, and as long as fire remains on the altar of God, glory is inevitable. Slaughtering shame is an easy adventure when the fire of the Holy Spirit is upheld. John the Baptist said,

> He [Jesus] shall baptize you with the Holy Spirit and with fire ... and thoroughly purge his floor, and will gather the wheat into his garner but the chaff he will burn with fire unquenchable. (Luke 3:16–17)

When heaven wants to change earth's landscape, fire is added. In Revelation 8:3–5, we read,

> There was given much incense, that he should offer it with the prayers of all saints upon the golden altar. And the smoke of the incense, which came with the prayers of the

saints, ascended up before God out of the angel's hand. And the angel took the censer, and filled it with fire of the altar, and cast it into the earth: and there were voices, and thunderings, and lightnings, and an earthquake.

The fire of the Lord changed the status quo of worship, praise, and prayer into earthquakes, thundering, and lightning voices. The effect of this kind of shaking is glory. Haggai 2:7 says, "I will shake all nations, and the desire of all nations shall come and I will fill this house with glory, saith the Lord of hosts."

Ichabod or Ignite?

Ichabod, meaning "the glory has departed," was what Eli's daughter-in-law named her son following the death of her husband, father-in-law, and brother-in-law in one day (1 Samuel 4:21).

The dearth of glory in Eli's era as high priest was not a sudden event but started when "the lamp of God went out in the temple of the Lord, where the ark of God was" (1 Samuel 3:3). When the fire of the Lord is out, the glory of God is nonexistent.

Elijah, on the other hand, called down fire from heaven (1 Kings 18:38), and the clouds released rain or glory that stopped a drought of three and a half years. His ministry climaxed with the slaughter of the shameful prophets of Baal (1 Kings 18:39–46) who had misled Israel.

Elijah represents the ignition fire of the Holy Spirit, while Eli represents the Ichabod spirit. Eli's descendants ended their lives in shame and ignominy (1 Samuel 2:31–36), while Elijah is returning in glory as the headline act of Jesus' last-day army (Malachi 4:5).

The choice we have as a generation is to be ignited by the power of the Holy Spirit or become the Ichabods of our generation. God's choice is stated in Hebrews 1:7: "His ministers are a flame of fire." Your platform for glory is established in the fire of the Holy Spirit.

Delivered by Fire

When the disciples were locked up, afraid, and ashamed after the death of Jesus (John 20:19), God sent the fire of the Holy Spirit, and their shame disappeared. Acts 2:2–4 says, "Suddenly there came a sound from heaven ... and there appeared unto them cloven tongues like as of fire and sat upon each of them. And they were all filled with the Holy Ghost."

The disciples went from bankrupt and broken to beautiful and bold after the baptism with the fire of the Holy Spirit. Acts 4:13 says, "When they saw the boldness of Peter and John, and perceived that they were unlearned and ignorant men, they marveled and took knowledge of them that they had been with Jesus."

Even their enemies could not deny the difference in the glory and grace upon their lives when the fire of the Lord fell in Acts 1. The apostle Peter, who had been scared by a maid (Mark 14:66–68) into denying Jesus, stood in front of thousands and preached a message that brought three thousand into the kingdom (Acts 2:41).

The transformation that occurred was not because Jesus had appeared to them again or had spoken words of hope to them but because they had received the fire of the Lord on Pentecost. Isaiah 33:14–17 says those who

> dwell with the devouring fire [or the] ... everlasting burnings ... shall dwell on high. His place of defense shall be the munitions of rocks and bread shall be given him. His waters shall be sure [and their] eyes shall see the king in his beauty [and] behold the land very far off.

The Fire of the Glory

Isaiah the prophet was ashamed at the altar. He had just lost his mentor, King Uzziah, and on beholding God's glory, said, "Woe is me for I am undone [and] am a man of unclean lips, and dwell in the midst of a people of unclean lips" (Isaiah 6:5).

His shame was a product of sin and self-centeredness. Its solution, however, was the fire of the Lord from the altar. Isaiah 6:6–7 says, "The seraphims [flew] unto me, having a live coal in his hand, which he had taken with the tongs from off the altar and laid it upon my mouth, and said, Lo, this hath touched thy lips and thine iniquity is taken away."

Whenever you want to stop shame, start a Holy Spirit fire. As 1 Corinthians 3:13 says, "Every man's work shall be made manifest for the day shall declare it, because it shall be revealed by fire and the fire shall try every man's work of what sort it is."

Whoever wants to see the Lord in His glory must maintain the fire of the glory on the altar. Leviticus 6:13 says, "The fire shall ever be burning upon the altar [and] it shall never go out." The fire of the Holy Spirit is the ingredient for renewing the glory of God. Psalm 29:7–9 says,

> The voice of the Lord divides the flames of fire. The voice of the Lord shakes the wilderness [and] shakes the wilderness of Kadesh. The voice of the Lord makes the hinds to calve, and discovers the forests and in his temple doth every one speak of his glory.

One More Million

Steve Hill (1954-2014) is best known as the evangelist who preached at the Brownsville Revival in Pensacola, Florida, in the 1990s. During that time, he saw a move of God that drew more than four million from around the world and saved hundreds of thousands of people.

In 2011, Hill was given up for dead by the medical community. He had an aggressive, stage-IV malignant melanoma that had spread to his bones. After several years of chemotherapy and surgical treatments, he was given days to live. He could not remember his wife's name and was not aware of his surroundings.

While on his deathbed, he told his wife, Jeri, to take him off all his medications. Jeri was advised against it, but she listened to her husband and the Lord. In what looked like his last days on earth, with his last ounce of strength, Hill prayed a prayer that changed his circumstances: "Jesus, you have a choice. We're best friends, Lord, and I trust you. You can either take my life and let me die, which the Bible says is gain, or you could let me live and I will win another million souls to you."

After this vow of a prayer, Hill made a supernatural recovery. He underwent medical and holistic therapy and eighteen months later, he is healthier than he was while undergoing chemotherapy. He went headlong into his mission of adding another million souls to the kingdom of God by being featured in numerous evangelistic and ministry outreaches. He died in faith on March 9th 2014 having fulfilled his agreement with God.

You are the greatest prophet to your own life.

Chapter Twenty-Five

Slaughtering Shame: The Fruit of Our Lips

Sound speech, that cannot be condemned that he that is of the contrary
part may be ashamed, having no evil thing to say of you.
—Titus 2:8

What you said is why you are shamed as a Christian. Shame has no place in the Christian wardrobe, but if your words are ensnaring your life, you will reap the consequences. Proverbs 6:2 says, "Thou art snared with the words of thy mouth, thou art taken with the words of thy mouth." Your words do not go unnoticed by heaven and can cause shame or glory to be manifested in your life.

Proverbs 18:20–21 says, "A man's belly shall be satisfied with the fruit of his mouth and with the increase of his lips shall he be filled. Death and life are in the power of the tongue and they that love it shall eat the fruit thereof." It is what "ye bind on earth [that] shall be bound in heaven and what ye loose on earth that shall be loosed in heaven" (Matthew 18:18). The fruit of our lips can shape the glory or shame our life manifests.

Proverbs 13:2–3 cautions us: "A man shall eat good by the fruit of his mouth but the soul of the transgressors shall eat violence. He that keeps his mouth keeps his life but he that opens wide his lips shall have destruction."

The Power of Praise

The most important reason God gave you a mouth was to praise Him. Anything less than virtue and praise from your mouth is defiling your temple. James 3:6 says, "The tongue is a fire, a world of iniquity: so is the tongue among our members, that it defiles the whole body, and sets on fire the course of nature."

We are created to praise God; Revelation 4:11 says, "Thou art worthy, O Lord, to receive glory and honor and power for thou hast created all things, and for thy pleasure they are and were created." The churches' abrogation of this responsibility has caused shame to camouflage its otherwise glorious destiny.

Hebrews 13:15 says, "Let us offer the sacrifice of praise to God continually, that is, the fruit of our lips giving thanks to his name." Praise is not circumstantial but continuous, and as we walk in continuous praise, we build an aroma of His glory around us continually.

Proverbs 28:12a says, "When righteous men do rejoice, there is great glory but when the wicked rise, a man is hidden." When the righteous praise God, His presence envelopes us according to Psalm 22:3, and as we live a lifestyle of praise by praising Him continually (Psalm 34:1), we become a place for His glory to dwell. Isaiah 44:23 says,

> Sing, O ye heavens for the Lord hath done it: shout, ye lower
> parts of the earth: break forth into singing, ye mountains,
> O forest, and every tree therein: for the Lord hath redeemed
> Jacob, and glorified himself in Israel.

Shame departs when the praise of God is present. Glory replaces shame in the midst of praise and causes destinies to be changed. Psalm 67:5-6 says, "Let the people praise thee, O God; let all the people praise thee. Then shall the earth yield her increase and God, even our own God, shall bless us."

Don't Just Talk—Give Thanks

When we thank God, we turn the glory rain on. In 2 Corinthians 4:15, Paul said, "All things are for your sakes, that the abundant grace might through the thanksgiving of many redound to the glory of God."

On the other hand, when we curse or blaspheme God, we set shame in motion. As 1 Corinthians 10:10 says, "Neither murmur ye, as some of them also murmured, and were destroyed of the destroyer."

Rather than complain, God wants us to compliment others. Instead of always grumbling and telling others how bad things are, we are encouraged by God to be grateful and thank Him for what we already have.

Jeremiah 30:19 says, "Out of them shall proceed thanksgiving and the voice of them that make merry and I will multiply them and they shall not be few. I will also glorify them, and they shall not be small."

Where you end up in life depends on who you endeared yourself to by praise. God will glorify you when you speak with a voice of thanksgiving, but the world will shame you when you chronicle a catalogue of woes.

Satisfaction with good or glory in life starts with the fruit of the mouth called thanksgiving. Proverbs 12:14 says, "A man shall be satisfied with good by the fruit of his mouth and the recompense of a man's hands shall be rendered unto him."

Give God the Glory

Another way of ensuring the slaughter of shame is by giving glory to God. It ensures that the travesty of pride will be broken and God's presence will go with us. Malachi 2:2 says,

> If ye will not hear, and if ye will not lay it to heart, to give glory unto my name, saith the LORD of hosts, I will even send a curse upon you, and I will curse your blessings: yea, I have cursed them already, because ye do not lay it to heart.

Speak what glorifies God, and your body will never be a hindrance to God's glory in your life. James 3:2 says, "If any man offend not in word, the same is a perfect man, and able also to bridle the whole body."

Your boasting may be why your glory is blighted. Stop reveling in your achievements and revel in God's beneficence. Proverbs 27:1–2 says, "Boast not thyself of tomorrow for thou knows not what a day may bring forth. Let another man praise thee, and not thine own mouth; a stranger, and not thine own lips."

Always give God the glory with the fruit of your mouth. Proverbs 25:27–28 says, "It is not good to eat much honey: so for men to search their own glory is not glory. He that hath no rule over his own spirit is like a city that is broken down, and without walls."

When pride rules people's spirits and they deny the glory due to God, they will become sources of perennial shame. According to Proverbs 25, they will be broken and burnt without walls, symbolizing loss of defense and glory.

The Emancipation Movement

William Wilberforce (1759–1833) wanted nothing more than to dedicate his life to ending the scourge of the slave trade and human trafficking. As a member of the English Parliament, he was instrumental in bringing twenty-one bills to the floor of the House of Commons calling for the emancipation of all slaves and the abolition of slavery.

On twenty different occasions, he failed. His body was ravaged by disease and his finances were hurt by sanctions placed on his companies by the multinationals involved in the slave trade, but he persisted. He once said,

> So enormous, so dreadful, so irremediable did the [slave] trade's wickedness appear that my own mind was completely made up for abolition. Let the consequences be what they would: I from this time determined that I would never rest until I had effected its abolition.

Wilberforce saw the United Kingdom's abolition of slave trade in 1807, after more than twenty bills and twenty years of trying to change state policy. He died three days later, but he is best remembered for that singular legacy. He is buried in Westminster Abbey, the burial place of English kings and queens, and he was accorded a state burial as a reward for a life dedicated to one purpose—abolition.

You and I are God's greatest assets; Don't let sin make you a liability.

Chapter Twenty-Six

Slaughtering Shame: The Freedom of the Lord

Now the Lord is that Spirit and where the Spirit of the Lord is, there is liberty. But we all, with open face beholding as in a glass the glory of the Lord, are changed into the same image from glory to glory, even as by the Spirit of the Lord.
—2 Corinthians 3:17–18

Until we break the stronghold of bondage, glory will remain elusive. Bondage is not necessarily being in cells, chained down with shackles, but anything that controls you other than the Spirit of God. As 2 Peter 2:19 says, "They promise them liberty [but] they themselves are servants of corruption. For of whom a man is overcome, of the same is he brought in bondage."

Your appetites as a believer have been changed by the Spirit of God, and humanity cannot keep you in bondage against your will. You are no more a servant of sin but a slave to righteousness and holiness. Romans 6:18 says, "Being then made free from sin, ye became the servants of righteousness."

The church Jesus is coming for is a "glorious Church without spot or wrinkle" (Ephesians 5:27). It is not a church laden with bondage to sin but one that lives in the liberty of the Spirit and is transformed from shame to glory.

Living in liberty ensures that glory escalates in your life. Bondage to sin, on the other hand, dissolves that glory and stifles His presence.

James 1:25 says, "Whoso looks into the perfect law of liberty, and continues therein, he being not a forgetful hearer, but a doer of the work, this man shall be blessed in his deed."

The Power of Prudence

Proverbs 12:16 says, "A fool's wrath is presently known but a prudent man covers shame." To slaughter shame, you must empower prudence. The Hebrew word for *prudence*, as used in Proverbs 12:16, is *awroom*, which means "smoothness" or "bareness."

The gentleness of God makes for our greatness and glory, but the stubbornness of humanity causes its shame and struggles. Proverbs 29:1 says, "He, that being often reproved hardens his neck, shall suddenly be destroyed, and that without remedy."

A lot of believers stay in shame because they don't allow the Spirit of God smooth control of their spirits. They are hesitant and reluctant arbiters of God's will and miss out on the shameless glory He promises.

Upheld by Thy Free Spirit

In Psalm 51:12, David prayed, "Restore unto me the joy of thy salvation and uphold me with thy free spirit." The stifling of the Holy Spirit is the *primus inter pares* reason so many Christian centers of learning have become mortuaries instead of monasteries, cemeteries instead of seminaries.

You can't uphold the Holy Spirit; you must be upheld by Him to be turned from shame to glory. Psalm 119:116 says, "Uphold me according unto thy word that I may live and let me not be ashamed of my hope."

The Holy Spirit is likened to a wind in John 3:8, and He cannot be shortchanged, circumvented, or straightjacketed. He is also described as fire (Acts 2:3–4) and oil (Luke 4:18), and these symbols are impossible to limit.

Our Achilles' heel in the church has not been the gospel of liberty but the reining in of the spirit of liberty. Rather than curtailing the movement of the Holy Spirit, we should give Him free rein because we are never freer than when we are under His guidance.

We Christians are called not to bondage but to blessings; we are not called to liability but to liberty. Sin is our greatest albatross on the road to glory, and we must destroy it. Proverbs 13:5 says, "A righteous man hateth lying: but a wicked man is loathsome, and cometh to shame."

Breaking Bondages and a Lifetime of Shame

Many Christians stay in bondage at the peril of their divine glory. Isaiah 21:16 says, "Thus hath the LORD said unto me, within a year, according to the years of an hireling, and all the glory of Kedar shall fail."

The word *kedar* in the above verse describes the labor of a hireling and means "ashen" or "dark." It means that if a man approaches work like a hireling instead of a heir, the glory of that work will be darkened or dusky.

What keeps great employees working at great companies is not the charity concept but the chance of becoming part of something bigger than themselves. The mentality of heirs as opposed to that of hirelings leaves an unfailing glory in the work for years to come because heirs consider themselves part of the design. Galatians 4:1–7 says,

> The heir, as long as he is a child, differs nothing from a servant, though he be lord of all. He is under tutors and governors until the time appointed of the father even so we, when we were children, were in bondage under the elements of the world. And because ye are sons, God hath sent forth the Spirit of his Son into your hearts, crying, Abba, Father. Wherefore thou art no more a servant, but a son; and if a son, then an heir of God through Christ.

The solution to the shame of sin and the burden of bondage was the sending forth of the spirit of freedom and the liberation of our captivity. Romans 8:21 says, "The creature itself also shall be delivered from the bondage of corruption into the glorious liberty of the children of God."

Somalia versus Singapore

The country of Singapore sits at the top of free-economy indexes worldwide. It has minimal restrictions on business and has a thriving economy as a result. According to the Boston Consulting Group, the island had 188,000 millionaire households in 2011—slightly more than 17 percent of its resident households—which effectively means one in six homes has disposable private wealth of at least $1 million, and this excludes property, businesses, and luxury goods.

Singapore has the highest gross domestic product per capita in the world at $56,532, having overtaken Norway, the United States, Hong Kong, and Switzerland according to a 2012 wealth report by Knight Frank and Citi Private Bank. It is now considered the home of the rich and famous because of its low taxes, zero harassment from paparazzi or protesters, and low crime rate. Its spirit of freedom has worked in its favor.

Spiritually, Singapore has metamorphosed from a predominantly Buddhist nation to one that is 30 percent Christian. Its freedom of religion and economic expressions has made Singapore an investors' haven for several Christian ministries such as the Haggai institute, New Creation Church, and several other internationally renowned ministries.

Somalia, on the other hand, sits at the bottom of the economic index of nations. It comprises desert land in the horn of Africa that is bordered by the Indian Ocean, Ethiopia, Kenya, and Djibouti. It was ruled by the colonial French, British, and Italians, and it attained independence in June 1960, a year after Singapore did. Soon after independence, however, it disintegrated into ethnic chaos. A military putsch led by General Said Barre overthrew the militia that had assassinated the elected president. Barre conferred on himself authoritarian powers, and for twenty-one years, he ruled the nation with an iron fist.

He instituted socialist values anchored on Islamic beliefs. He changed the language of the nation to a rudimentary form of Arabic and mercilessly annihilated the opposition. He began wars with his neighbors, built the largest army in Africa, and spent wanton sums of money on Soviet ammunition.

With war raging on all fronts, Barre fled the country in 1991, and since then, Somalia has had no legitimate government. In early 2012, a central government was formed, but it has still not been recognized by the tribal warlords fighting for their independence.

Somalia has over the years due to its lack of spiritual and financial freedom become a breeding ground for pirates and terrorists. A splinter group of Al-Qaida called Al-Shabah has taken root in that country and has caused widespread violence and crime in their neighboring nations. Its Muslim majority repress Christians through the "apostasy act" that prevents change of religion.

Somalia is a prototypical failed state mired in political instability, extreme violence, and famine. Its lack of freedom stopped its restoration. Singapore, on the other hand, is now considered one of the newly developed economies of the world, and it achieved this through increased financial and religious liberty.

PART VI

Rewards of Shamelessness

*If you know what's hidden,
you will not be hidden in life.*

Chapter Twenty-Seven

Rewards of Shamelessness: Hidden Mysteries

That he would grant you, according to the riches of his glory, to be strengthened with might by his Spirit in the inner man. That Christ may dwell in your hearts by faith (and) that ye, being rooted and grounded in love ... (may) know the love of Christ, which passes knowledge (and) ye might be filled with all the fullness of God.
—Ephesians 3:16–18

The lives of Christians can be devoid of or full of glory depending on their knowledge of God. As 2 Peter 1:3–4 says, we have been given all things for life and godliness "through the knowledge of him that hath called us to glory and virtue whereby are given unto us exceeding great and precious promises that by these we might be partakers of the divine nature."

Our knowledge and understanding of the hidden will ensure that we are not hidden in life. The glory we radiate is dependent on the revelations we uncover. Proverbs 25:2 says, "It is the glory of God to conceal a thing but the honor of kings to search out a matter."

The difference between those who shine in life and those who live life ashamed is knowledge. Job said, "My glory was fresh in me, and my bow was renewed in my hand" when "the secret of God was upon my tabernacle" (Job 29:4).

The key to His glory are his great and precious promises and the solution to ministry matters is dependence on His mysteries.

Ignorance of them will send us to oblivion. Hosea 4:6 says, "My people are perished for lack of knowledge."

Because You Glow, You Know

In moments of conflict and confusion, glory makes the difference; it lights the path and dissolves darkness and doubt. John 1:5 says, "The light shines in darkness and the darkness comprehended it not."

The light of God's Word is our tool for disproving every shame thrown at us by Satan. Ephesians 5:12–13 says, "It is a shame even to speak of those things which are done of them in secret but all things that are reproved are made manifest by the light for whatsoever doth make manifest is light."

Light is the eternal solution to shame, but when we are ignorant, we live our lives in shame instead of His glory. Ephesians 3:16–18 teaches us that the glory of God spurs discovery that births destinies. Jesus was described by John the Baptist as "a light to lighten the Gentiles, and the glory of thy people Israel (Luke 2:32).

You cannot bring light and remain outside the glory. Jesus "increased in wisdom and stature, and in favor with God and man" (Luke 2:52). Favor is a prelude to glory, but it is first preceded by growth in wisdom.

From Glory to Glory—From Strength to Strength

Psalm 84:7 says, "They go from strength to strength, every one of them in Zion [who] appears before God." Until there is an appearance before God and His glory, strength cannot be increased.

Your strength represents your knowledge of the Word of God. Proverbs 26:20 says, "Where no wood is, there the fire goeth out," and Haggai 1:6 adjures us to "go up to the mountain, and bring wood, and build the house; and I will take pleasure in it, and I will be glorified."

Ignominy starts with ignorance, but shame stops with studying God's Word. Until the mysteries of the kingdom are revealed, solutions to shame are not available.

I Am Having the Time of My Life

I was sent by God to Gimbie, Ethiopia, as a medical missionary with Adventist Health International in September 2004. I had successfully defended my master's degree thesis in medical parasitology at the University of London after a six-week practicum in Zanzibar, and I was expected to settle into the Western world's sophisticated medical system.

Contrary to all expectations, I chose to go to Ethiopia, a posting that offered no salaries or allowances; it provided only airfare for my wife and me and accommodation at a seventy-bed hospital in Wellagoa District in the country.

During our time there, my wife and I pioneered Friday night all-night prayer meetings, visited prisons, and preached in several Bible-believing churches in the area.

While working as the primary-care physician in the town and assisting the chief surgeon with surgeries, I could hear myself muttering the words of a well-known song, "I am having the time of my life and I never felt this way before."

At the end of those three months in Gimbie, I was offered a surgical residency in a New York hospital easily. Until today, my wife tells anyone who cares to listen that those three months in Gimbie were the best months of her life. God is faithful, but we must be faithful to His will first.

They cannot do what you know until they know what you do.

Chapter Twenty-Eight

Rewards of Shamelessness: Holiness

Christ also loved the church, and gave himself for it that he might sanctify and cleanse it with the washing of water by the word, that he might present it to himself a glorious church, not having spot, or wrinkle, or any such thing; but that it should be holy and without blemish.
—Ephesians 5:25–27

Shame is synonymous with sin, while holiness is synonymous with glory. Exodus 15:11 says, "Who is like unto thee, O LORD, among the gods? Who is like thee, glorious in holiness, fearful in praises, doing wonders?"

The church that walks in the glory of God will be holy and pure. Ephesians 5:27 says God is coming for a glorious church "not having spot, or wrinkle, or any such thing; but that it should be holy and without blemish."

The last-days church is a glorious church, not a garbage church. It is holy and without blemish because of the glory of God upon her. Proverbs 4:18 says, "The path of the just is as the shining light, that shineth more and more unto the perfect day." Perfection is the end point when glory is shining en route to that destination. In Haggai 2:9, the Lord said, "The glory of this latter house shall be greater than of the former, saith the LORD of hosts and in this place will I give peace, saith the LORD of hosts."

Holiness is equivalent to peace with God; according to Romans 5:1, we are "justified [made righteous] by faith [and so] have peace with God through our Lord Jesus Christ." When there is glory in the house, peace is the result.

Samuel: The Power of Integrity

Samuel was a man of integrity and justice. He asked the children of Israel,

> Witness against me before the LORD, and before his anointed: whose ox have I taken? or whose ass have I taken? or whom have I defrauded? whom have I oppressed? or of whose hand have I received any bribe to blind mine eyes therewith?" to which the people replied "thou hast not defrauded us, nor oppressed us, neither hast thou taken ought of any man's hand" (1 Samuel 12:4).

In the midst of wanton corruption and diabolical waywardness, Samuel stood out for righteousness. The secret to his purity of lifestyle and uprightness was, however, the shameless and frank relationship he had with God.

While the rest of the people were living in spiritual oblivion (1 Samuel 3:1), Samuel had daily encounters with God that bolstered his integrity. In 1 Samuel 3:21, we read, "The LORD appeared again in Shiloh for the LORD revealed himself to Samuel in Shiloh by the word of the LORD."

It was this glory of unashamed communion with God that strengthened Samuel to stand unflinchingly for righteousness. In 1 Samuel 12:23, he told the people of Israel, "God forbid that I should sin against the LORD in ceasing to pray for you but I will teach you the good and the right way." Until you get a glimpse of His glory, sin cannot become an anathema to you.

Isaiah: The Power of Shameless Glory

What the world needs is a revelation of Christ's glory to change humanity's heart. That revelation of glory will result in pure living. For example, the prophet Isaiah said, "Woe is me! for I am undone because I am a man of unclean lips, and I dwell in the midst of a people of unclean lips for mine eyes have seen the King, the Lord of hosts" (Isaiah 6:5).

The manifestation of God's glory resulted in the prophet Isaiah's repentance and a purging of sin in his life. Isaiah 6:7 says, "Upon my mouth, this [hot coal] touched thy lips and my iniquity is taken away and my sin [is] purged."

Before Isaiah saw the Lord, he had a shameful or masked appearance in God's appearance. In spite of his position and eloquence as a prophet, Isaiah was living ashamed. He had a life controlled by the power of King Uzziah (Isaiah 6:1), and only after Uzziah died did he see the glory of God.

Shamelessness is not in titles, positions, or pedigrees but in an unfettered, explicit relationship with our Master and Lord Jesus Christ. Don't let people stop you from beholding God's glory; if you do, holiness may elude you forever.

My Publication's Story

I graduated as the best graduating resident in family medicine from my program. To my credit, I wrote almost twenty scientific publications in my three years of residency and had successfully developed a department with a knack in that area.

My adventure with publishing, however, started with persistence and an unwavering passion in pursuit of a cause. Even though New York State had started the implementation of the Libby Zion Law, making medical residents subject to an eighty-hour work week, I entered a surgical case post-call voluntarily.

I followed the patient for two years till he died. By the time the article I wrote about his case was published in a peer-reviewed journal, I had visited his house, had met his widow, had introduced myself to the extended family, and had my professional article rejected multiple times by several scientific journals.

Life never hands out victory without violence; as Jesus said in Matthew 11:12, "From the days of John the Baptist until now the Kingdom of Heaven suffers violence, and the violent take it by force." I took it by violence and obtained the victory as a result.

*There is no high like
the most high.*

Chapter Twenty-Nine

Rewards of Shamelessness: Healing

According to my earnest expectation and my hope, that in nothing I shall
be ashamed, but that with all boldness, as always, so now also Christ
shall be magnified in my body, whether it be by life, or by death.
—Philippians 1:20

The burden of disease and sickness has never been greater. Current estimates project that more than 10 percent of the world's population of 600 million have diabetes, more than 300 million are crippled, more than 50 million are blind, more than 40 million have died of HIV/AIDS, and depression affects around 350 million people worldwide. Cancer is expected to become the world's number-one killer by 2015, overtaking cardiovascular disease for the prime spot. This has occurred in an environment encouraged by obesity, smoking, lack of exercise, and poor lifestyle practices.

The panacea to this wanton destruction is the glory of God. When the sun of righteousness arises, healing is sure. Malachi 4:2 says, "Unto you that fear my name shall the Sun of righteousness arise with healing in his wings and ye shall go forth and grow up as calves of the stall."

God's will for us is not that we become sick or diseased but that we glorify God in our bodies by walking as the healed of the Lord. As

1 Corinthians 6:20 says, "Ye are bought with a price: therefore glorify God in your body, and in your spirit, which are God's."

Sickness does not glorify God but is rather a shame to the body. Jesus came to destroy sickness, sin, and sorrow. Isaiah 53:4–5 says Jesus

> hath borne our griefs, and carried our sorrows ... But he was wounded for our transgressions, he was bruised for our iniquities: the chastisement of our peace was upon him; and with his stripes we are healed.

Moses: Power at One Hundred and Twenty

Moses was as strong at age 120 as he was when he was 40. "Moses was a hundred and twenty years old when he died; his eye was not dim nor his natural force abated" (Deuteronomy 34:7). Moses' unprecedented strength was due to the glory and unashamed interaction he had with God. Twice while on forty-day fasts (Exodus 24:18, 34:28), Moses saw the glory of God so much so "that the skin of his face shone while God talked to him" (Exodus 34:29).

This glory acted as a deterrent to sickness and disease and renewed his strength. Rather than grow weaker, his body grew stronger and more glorious. The secret to his longevity and agility was the glory of God. The apostle Paul said in 2 Corinthians 4:15–16, "Redound to the glory of God for which cause we faint not but though our outward man perish yet the inward man is renewed day by day."

The glory of God will multiply your strength. While three to six million contemporaries of Moses died in the wilderness, Moses lived on in strength and health because he saw the glory.

The Bible says in Exodus 33:18 that Moses prayed to God, "Show me thy glory," and God said, "I will make all my goodness pass before thee and I will proclaim the name of the Lord before thee" (Exodus 33:19). The life Moses had at age 120 stemmed from his glorious meetings with God.

The Power of God to Heal

Healing takes place every time the glory is present. The Bible says, "There were Pharisees and doctors of the law sitting by, which were come out of every town of Galilee, and Judaea, and Jerusalem and the power of the Lord was present to heal them."

Wherever the glory is present, healing occurs. The Bible says,

> The Lord will create upon every dwelling place of mount Zion, and upon her assemblies, a cloud and smoke by day, and the shining of a flaming fire by night for upon all the glory shall be a defense. (Isaiah 4:6)

God's glory is a defense in times of danger and a canopy in times of covert satanic activities. Isaiah 58:8 says, "Thine health shall spring forth speedily and thy righteousness shall go before thee [and] the glory of the Lord shall be thy reward." What the world needs is not more medications or man-made methods to heal but the glory of God. When the glory is your defense, it covers even what you don't know about (that is rearguard), and healing occurs rapidly.

Uma Ukpai and the Witches' Curse

Dr. Oguine, an obstetrician/gynecologist in Aba, Nigeria, had just finished operating on a woman in her midforties when he suddenly became paralyzed. He lost movement in the right side of his body and went dumb.

The woman he had operated on was a self-confessed witch and had warned him not to operate on her if he wanted to live. He had ignored her warning, concerned that her massive vaginal bleeding would cost her her life.

He was a nominal churchgoer at that point, and after Dr. Uma Ukpai and other men of God ministered to him, he was restored to full health. Two weeks later, however, the witch called him, and after speaking to her, his symptoms reappeared.

He went to the best rehabilitation and neurological physicians in the country, but no one could ameliorate much less improve his condition. He rapidly went downhill and, two years after the commencement of this malaise, he turned his heart to Jesus asking for forgiveness of sins and healing.

He became an ardent student of the Word of God, and he eventually regained use of the right side of his body. His speech was restored, and he was able to perform surgeries again. The curse of stroke had been broken by the power in the name of Jesus.

Where the river of God flows, the buildings never fail.

Chapter Thirty

Rewards of Shamelessness: Honor

Poverty and shame shall be to him that refuseth instruction
but he that regards reproof shall be honored.
—Proverbs 13:18

The man or woman who refuses to be ashamed at the altar or in life will be honored in the life to come. Mark 8:38 says,

> Whosoever therefore shall be ashamed of me and of my words in this adulterous and sinful generation; of him also shall the Son of man be ashamed, when he cometh in the glory of his Father with the holy angels.

Our life's worth is not in the accolades of men or the garlands of nations but in our recognition at God's throne. As 1 Corinthians 3:12–15 tells us,

> Every man's work shall be made manifest for the day shall declare it because it shall be revealed by fire and the fire shall try every man's work of what sort it is. If any man's work abide which he hath built thereupon, he shall receive a reward. If any man's work shall be burned, he shall suffer loss: but he himself shall be saved; yet so as by fire.

What we build in life will be burned up and suffer loss and shame or abide the fire and receive a reward. Some, as will be the case with those who suffer loss, will enter heaven ashamed and so will not be honored because they did not embrace a shameless, spiritual life devoid of artificiality. A shameless life builds eternal investments, and heaven will honor them on their arrival.

Enemies at the Gate

Psalm 127:4–5 says,

> As arrows are in the hand of a mighty man so are children of the youth. Happy is the man that hath his quiver full of them: they shall not be ashamed, but they shall speak with the enemies in the gate.

Enemies at the gate have the potential to cause shame if they defeat you. In Old Testament culture, a gate symbolized authority and honor. For example, Job said he "went out to the gate through the city [and] prepared his seat in the street. The young men saw him and hid themselves and the aged arose, and stood up" (Job 29:7–8).

A man who, while facing his enemies at the gate, has his quiver full of arrowlike sons is never ashamed. They face the battles of life unashamed and so become honorable men. Every one of us faces enemies at the gates of our lives, and the outcome can be defeat or honor. The size of your enemies doesn't determine your victory but the estimation of your glory. If you come to spiritual war ashamed, intimidated, and insecure, you will be destroyed and doomed to perpetual shame, but if you come in the glory of your seed, victory is undeniable.

Breaking Dishonor

The only solution to dishonor is honor. Until you live by honor, you will remain dishonorable in life. As 1 Samuel 2:30 says, "Be it far from me for them that honor me I will honor, and they that despise me shall be lightly esteemed."

Mephibosheth, the son of Jonathan and a grandson of King Saul, was abandoned by the leaders of Israel after his father's and grandfather's demise because he was considered shameful. Lame at a young age, orphaned, and derelict in a town called Lodebar (meaning "no pasture"), he had nothing to look forward to (2 Samuel 9).

His name, however, was his source of breakthrough. Mephibosheth means "shame destroyer" or "image breaker," and King David, in recognition of his covenant with Jonathan, took Mephibosheth, and he "ate at his table, as one of the king's sons" (2 Samuel 9:11b). David turned Mephibosheth's shame into glory by bringing him into an unashamed, unhindered relationship with David. The result of this unfettered access was glory that made for a restoration of Mephibosheth's honor. In 2 Samuel 9:7, King David said to Mephisbosheth, "I will restore all the land of Saul thy father and thou shalt eat bread at my table continually."

The life of glory and shamelessness promotes one to honor, but a life of shame and despair over the past leads to dishonor. Jesus said, "How can ye believe, which receive honor one of another, and seek not the honor that comes from God only?" (John 5:44).

Until our priority is Him and we burn the bridges of the past and stand on the stones of the Word alone, honor remains elusive. As 1 Chronicles 16:27 says, "Glory and honor are in his presence; strength and gladness are in his place."

From Shame to Fame

Pastor Matthew Ashimolowo was vilified and slandered following a report on his financial management of his church – the Kingsway International Christian center (KICC). Stories saying he had relocated to avoid preying eyes began to make the rounds in the United Kingdom.

The government took possession of the church's ten-acre property as the major site for the 2012 London Olympics and denied the church equitable land in exchange. For six years, Pastor Matthew and his congregation had to hold seven services per week in a London cinema that sat less than a thousand.

Eventually, their prayers were answered. A bid for a twenty-four-acre property in a nearby London suburb was accepted at 10 percent of its original value. The payment was made freehold, cash down, and debt free.

The champions of KICC, who were deemed homeless and hapless by naysayers, are now domiciled in a state-of-the-art, 7,000-capacity auditorium and a campus that consists of twelve free-standing facilities suitable for offices and Bible school training.

Pastor Matthew has gone from shame to fame. He has become the toast of the religious elite worldwide for his patience, persistence, and power with God to deliver such glory. The site is aptly named Prayer City, and it has elevated the honor of the church in England.

God is the anointer without number.

Chapter Thirty-One

Rewards of Shamelessness: Home of Blessings

They shall not be ashamed in the evil time: and in the
days of famine they shall be satisfied.
—Psalm 37:19

Your supply is determined by your shamelessness. In the days of famine, according to Psalm 37:19, you will be favored and flourish instead of being famished. The shameless Christian goes from glory to glory, but the ashamed believer descends into oblivion. As 2 Corinthians 3:18 says, "We all, with open face beholding as in a glass the glory of the Lord, are changed into the same image from glory to glory, even as by the Spirit of the Lord."

Your end will be greater than your beginning when the spirit of shameless faith and intimate communion resides in you. Psalm 84:7 says, "They go from strength to strength, every one of them in Zion [who] appears before God."

Glory Will Herald a Wealth Transfer

In Haggai 2:7–9, the Lord said,

> He will shake all nations, and the desire of all nations shall
> come and He will fill this house with glory [and with] the

silver ... and the gold [for] the glory of this latter house shall be greater than of the former.

According to Proverbs 13:22, before the wealth of the heathen is brought into the church, there will be a shaking of all that is shakeable and the glory of God will be revealed. When that happens, the wealth of the wicked can be transferred into the hands of the church.

The last-days church is a glorious church (Ephesians 5:27), and it will be distinguished by its wealth for the end-time harvest. Isaiah 60:2–5 says,

> The LORD shall arise upon thee, and his glory shall be seen upon thee. And the Gentiles shall come to thy light, and kings to the brightness of thy rising ... Then thou shalt see, and flow together, and thine heart shall fear, and be enlarged because the abundance of the sea shall be converted unto thee [and] the forces of the Gentiles shall come unto thee.

When the world sees our glory, its people will give heed to us. For example, Exodus 11:3 says, "The LORD gave the people favor in the sight of the Egyptians. Moreover the man Moses was very great in the land of Egypt, in the sight of Pharaoh's servants, and in the sight of the people."

The greatness or glory of Moses in the eyes of the Egyptians kickstarted the wealth transfer from the Egyptians to the Israelites that jumpstarted their economy. Tomorrow's blessing is hinged on today's glory.

When the Queen of Sheba saw the glory of Solomon's temple, "there was no more spirit in her" (1 Kings 10:5) and "she gave [Solomon] an hundred and twenty talents of gold, and of spices very great store, and precious stones" (1 Kings 10:10). To see tomorrow's gold, walk in today's glory.

A Double Dip for Disgrace

Isaiah 61:6–7a says, "Ye shall eat the riches of the Gentiles, and in their glory shall ye boast yourselves [and] for your shame ye shall have double." For every stroke of shame suffered from captivity, God has given a promise of double blessing. The Bible adds in Isaiah 61:7b that "in their land ye shall possess the double, [and] everlasting joy shall be unto them."

God turns around disgrace or shame when we are unashamed in His presence to such a degree that even the heathen acknowledge His glory and deliverance. Isaiah 61:9 says these unashamed ones will have "their seed ... known among the Gentiles, offspring among the people, [and] all that see them shall acknowledge them [as] the seed which the LORD hath blessed."

The adornment of glory and the withdrawal of shame is part of the finished death, burial, and resurrection of Jesus on the cross. It is a right, not a privilege. Every believer is blessed and has become a home of blessing by the work of Jesus on Calvary.

As 2 Corinthians 8:9 says, "Ye know the grace of our Lord Jesus Christ, that, though he was rich, yet for your sakes he became poor, that ye through his poverty might be rich."

Mart Green's Story

Mart Green is the Oklahoma-based billionaire and chief executive of Mardel and Hobby Lobby. A born-again Christian, he has been in the forefront of fulfilling the gospel's message in films, media, and books. He has single-handedly sponsored crusades to the Third World, produced films from a Christian viewpoint, and supported causes that have made him an important benefactor of institutions such as Oral Roberts University (ORU).

His parents and grandparents were not very wealthy, but Mart remembers his grandmother tithing everything that came her way—from clothes to food and money. She was a faithful witness for the cause of Christ and never failed to send missionary support offerings.

What she did left a lasting impression on young Mart, and he started tithing from the onset of his company. Hobby Lobby currently gives over 50 percent of its earnings to ministries across the world and has the record of giving the largest Christian philanthropic gift—$110 million—to ORU in 2010.

Green and his family are regular Sunday-school teachers at an Assembly of God church in Oklahoma and reserve forty days a year to fast and pray for their companies.

The result has been unprecedented growth and glory. The company has annual income of nearly $4 billion and has 573-plus stores in the United States that employ tens of thousands. They hold the torch of Jesus Christ in the marketplace. The company honors Sunday as a worship day by closing its stores, and it encourages family life by shutting shops at 8:00 p.m.

There can be no real success without a successor.

Chapter Thirty-Two

Rewards of Shamelessness: Heritage

*In their glory shall ye boast yourselves. For your shame ye shall have
double ... and their seed shall be known among the Gentiles, and their
offspring among the people: all that see them shall acknowledge
them, that they are the seed which the Lord hath blessed.*
—Isaiah 61:6,7, 9

Barnes Family research teaches that more than 70 percent of teenagers walk away from the Christian faith by the time they graduate college. They come from single-parent homes more than half the time, and the majority have experienced the occult, sex, incarceration, or drugs by the time they turn eighteen.

The shame covering this generation can be overcome by the glory of an unfettered walk with Jesus. Those children who once shamed you, according to God's Word, will become a veritable seed to save your coming generations.

The prophet Isaiah declares, "I and the children whom the Lord hath given me are for signs and for wonders" (Isaiah 8:18). Our children are a product of our relationship with God. If it is unashamed, we bring forth godly seed, but if it parochial and superficial, it can stifle them and leave them ill equipped to fight the battles of the now. In Isaiah 49:22–23, 25 God said,

I will lift up mine hand to the Gentiles, and set up my standard to the people: and they shall bring thy sons in their arms, and thy daughters shall be carried upon their shoulders. And kings shall be thy nursing fathers, and their queens thy nursing mothers ... for they shall not be ashamed that wait for me ... for I will contend with him that contends with thee, and I will save thy children.

Isaiah 54:4, 13 says,

Fear not; for thou shalt not be ashamed: neither be thou confounded; for thou shalt not be put to shame: for thou shalt forget the shame of thy youth, and shalt not remember the reproach of thy widowhood any more ... and all thy children shall be taught of the Lord; and great shall be the peace of thy children.

If this generation will be saved, let us stop shame in the church. We must forget our past shame and press on into the glory God has destined for the church.

Abraham: Anointing for Change

The seed of Abraham, according to Genesis 22:18, will bless all the nations of the earth. This happened because one man, Abraham, had an unashamed relationship with God. In Genesis 18:17–19, God said,

Shall I hide from Abraham that thing which I do; Seeing that Abraham shall surely become a great and mighty nation, and all the nations of the earth shall be blessed in him? For I know him, that he will command his children and his household after him.

Abraham had an inner-court interaction with God, and so His seed was blessed. His heritage is blessed because through one man, Abraham, they broke through the veil and developed a personal, intimate, and unashamed relationship with God the Father.

The word *Lot* means "veil" or "covering," and as long as Lot remained with Abraham, he was ashamed or covered in his relationship with God. When Lot and Abraham parted ways, however, God told Abraham to "lift up thine eyes, and look from the place where thou art northward, southward, eastward, and westward for all the land which thou sees, to thee will I give it, and to thy seed for ever" (Genesis 13:14–15).

The anointing for supernatural overflow and destiny correction for Abraham's seed started when he took the veil of Lot from his face. Today, Abraham is considered the father of faith (Genesis 4:11) and our reference for blessings (Galatians 3:14). His legacy and heritage continue because he went without the veil.

Elisha: Carrying His Heritage to the Grave

The prophet Elisha went to his grave brokenhearted and ashamed. As 2 Kings 13:14 says, "Elisha was fallen sick of his sickness whereof he died." Some commentators believe Elisha died unfulfilled because his servant, Gehazi, could not see the spiritual and ended up ashamed."

For example, Gehazi and his family ended up ostracized lepers because of his greed. As 2 Kings 5:27 says, "the leprosy therefore of Naaman shall cleave unto thee [Gehazi], and unto thy seed for ever." Gehazi lacked spiritual perception (2 Kings 6:17) and power with God (2 Kings 4:31). He eventually bequeathed a legacy of shame to his seed because he had a shamed or veiled relationship with God.

Eventually, Elisha, who had an honest relationship with God, took that anointing for change and deliverance to the grave. His shameless life had to touch earth some way with a heritage. We read in 2 Kings 13:21,

> As they were burying a man, behold, they spied a band of men; and they cast the man into the sepulchre of Elisha and when the man was let down, and touched the bones of Elisha, he revived, and stood up on his feet.

The fire of glory in Elisha's bones rattled the bones of this corpse till that man rose again. Elisha refused to die without bequeathing a heritage to his coming generations. There is a blessing in you for the world; don't die with it but let it out.

Dying Desperate and Desolate

My father's enterprises have a motley staff. As one of the directors and a medical staff of the company clinic, I was called on a particular day because one of our staff was in the hospital.

This staff had worked in the bar/restaurant for about a year and had been diagnosed with HIV in our clinic. She was promiscuous and a philanderer and was well known in the community for changing sex partners regularly.

She was screaming in agony in her bed at the clinic. Her words were incomprehensible, and her emotions irrepressible. She shook with every sob she took and was nothing more than a gathering of bones when I saw her.

Her heritage had been destroyed by shameful living. She had no one to call on, and as she died, there was no one but the medical personnel to comfort her. Her millionaire boyfriends, her family, and her unborn children were nowhere near.

Rather, death was near, and its angry and vicious claws soon took her to a place of no return. I attempted to preach the gospel to her in those last few minutes and hoped she received the mercy only Jesus could give. She prayed the sinners' prayer with her dying breadth, but all I could say in the end was what a shame. What a shame!

God has no favorites; just those who fear Him and those who don't.

Chapter Thirty-Three

Rewards of Shamelessness: Home to God

And ye shall know that I am in the midst of Israel, and that I am the Lord your God, and none else: and my people shall never be ashamed. And it shall come to pass afterward, that I will pour out my spirit upon all flesh.
—Joel 2:27–28

God will make His habitation where the believer is unashamed and has a frank relationship with Him. As 2 Corinthians 3:18 says, "But we all, with open face beholding as in a glass the glory of the Lord, are changed into the same image from glory to glory, even as by the Spirit of the Lord."

Those who draw near to God in faith are those He draws near to. Jeremiah 29:13 says, "Ye shall seek me, and find me, when ye shall search for me with all your heart." Those with relationships with God that have torn away the veil allow the Master to make their temples the habitation of the Spirit.

Psalm 91:1 says, "He that dwelleth in the secret place of the most High shall abide under the shadow of the Almighty." You cannot dwell in the secret place or be a home for God until you abide or come into his presence unashamed.

Expectation: Catalyst for the Glory

Philippians 1:20 says,

> According to my earnest expectation and my hope, that in
> nothing I shall be ashamed, but that with all boldness, as
> always, so now also Christ shall be magnified in my body,
> whether it be by life, or by death. For to me to live is Christ,
> and to die is gain.

Shame abrogates expectation. It makes the person who is ashamed feel unwanted and unaccepted, so that person can't approach God. Hebrews 4:16 says, "Let us therefore come boldly unto the throne of grace, that we may obtain mercy, and find grace to help in time of need."

We read in 1 Timothy 2:8, "I will that men everywhere lift up holy hands without wrath or doubting." Prayer is good, but if it is done with wrath or doubt, it's a fruitfulness exercise. It might be aerobics or a temple dance, but it is not unashamed communion with God.

A lifestyle of expectation in prayer is a lifestyle of glory. Proverbs 23:18 says, "Surely there is an end and thine expectation shall not be cut off." Shame builds a wall before the expected end, making your hands weak and unable to lift them or your face up before God.

The Fullness of the Godhead

In Ephesians 3:16, 19, we read,

> He would grant you, according to the riches of his glory, to
> be strengthened with might by his Spirit in the inner man ...
> and to know the love of Christ, which passeth knowledge,
> that ye might be filled with all the fulness of God.

Until the church goes beyond the veil and pursues glory, it will keep struggling for relevance in a hyped-up world. The Bible teaches us that the riches of His glory are the entrance point to being filled with God.

There is no minimum or maximum Christian. We are all called to the fullness of Christ according to Ephesians 3:19, and "herein is our love made perfect, that we may have boldness in the day of judgment: because as he is, so are we in this world" (1 John 4:17).

Every believer is called to be "a partaker of His divine nature" (2 Peter 1:4). As creatures "created in His image and likeness" (Genesis 1:26), we have no reason to walk in shame. The dilemma to our divinity on earth is perennial shame and a lack of understanding of our riches in His glory.

Safe in the Father's Arms

I was in medical school when the Christian medical and dental students at my university went to Port Harcourt (in Southern Nigeria) for a national conference. It was supposed to be a two-hour trip, but because of bad roads, poor logistics, and a bus that broke down several times, we were on the road until the wee hours of the night.

As we traveled, we were praising God. When we encountered an armed band that had been robbing wayfarers, some of our leaders talked with the robbers and explained we were students on a mission, and they let us go.

On arrival the next morning, sixteen hours later, we learned that those robbers had robbed, raped, and pillaged several travelers before we had come along; we were fortunate to have escaped unscathed. The atmosphere of praise and prayer we had on that bus had made us impregnable to satanic plots.

PART VII

Restoring a Generation

*Moderation is not
mediocrity.*

Chapter Thirty-Four

From Shame to Shekinah

To whom God would make known what is the riches of the glory of this
mystery among the Gentiles; which is Christ in you, the hope of glory.
—Colossians 1:27

What limits the church is not iniquity as much as intimidation. Shame has become commonplace and easily accepted in the church today, while glory has become an exceptional achievement instead of a daily pursuit accessible to every Christian by the blood of Jesus.

The Hebrew word *shekinah* describes a visible manifestation of divine presence. According to 2 Corinthians 3:7–9,

> If the ministration of death, written and engraven in stones, was glorious, so that the children of Israel could not stedfastly behold the face of Moses for the glory of his countenance; which glory was to be done away: How shall not the ministration of the spirit be rather glorious? For if the ministration of condemnation be glory, much more doth the ministration of righteousness exceed in glory.

Glory is our dwelling place, our status quo. Living in the glory must become our heavenly habit and not an earthly extreme. Isaiah 4:5 says, "the LORD will create upon every dwelling place of mount Zion, and upon her assemblies, a cloud and smoke by day, and the shining of a flaming fire by night: for upon all the glory shall be a defense."

From Shame to Glory in Seven Days

After seven days of being shamed for disputing the authority of Moses, Miriam was released from isolated captivity. In Numbers 12:14, God said, "If her father had but spit in her face, should she not be ashamed seven days? Let her be shut out from the camp seven days, and after that let her be received in again."

While she was shut out in the wilderness, ashamed with leprosy, Israel remained in Hazeroth. After seven days, however, "the people removed from Hazeroth, and pitched in the wilderness of Paran" (Numbers 12:16).

Hazeroth in the original Hebrew means "enclosed" but *Paran* means "ornaments." What formed barriers to destiny actualization can be traced to a father's shame. Shame makes you feel inadequate and unable to do what you otherwise could do, and it puts a ceiling on your capacity to dream. Anyone who wants to move from shame to glory, even when that shame is a product of a father's culpability, will do so, but only after seven days! Seven represents a complete makeover, and for the glory to return, there must be a complete surrender to the lordship of the Master and His Word in our lives.

Surrender: The Master Key to Glory

In Psalm 3:3, David described God as "a shield [and] my glory and the lifter up of mine head." If you want God to be the source of your glory, He must first be your shield. The word *shield*, as used in Psalm 3:3, refers to the sovereignty of God, and until we give free reign to the sovereign One who "holds up all things by the word of His Power" (Hebrews 1:3), we cannot taste the glory of God that lifts up our head.

The reason glory is elusive and at best episodic and epileptic in the church is because we have not fully surrendered all to Jesus. When we surrender all, the Lord becomes our glory, and our lifting continues instead of stalls.

Israel moved from its enclosed place (Hazeroth) to its glorified and overflowing place (Paran) after seven days of shame (Numbers

12:14–16). Shame that undergoes seven (meaning "complete" or "full") days of spiritual makeover is shame terminated and glory inhabited.

In John 12:24, Jesus said, "Except a corn of wheat fall into the ground and die, it abides alone but if it die it brings forth much fruit." The glory is in surrendering to God and not in struggling with God.

D. L. Moody—I Will Be the Man

D. L. Moody told a contemporary, after making a commitment to Jesus in his twenties, "The world has yet to see what God will do with, and for, and through, and in, and by the man who is fully consecrated to him ... and by God's grace, may I be that man!"

Born in 1837, he lived to age sixty-two and left footprints in the sand that are still there today. He pioneered Christian schools for boys and girls, encouraged interdenominational ministry, emphasized outreach to the marginalized and homeless, and equipped more than 50,000 Moody Bible School graduates even though he had only a fifth-grade education.

He gave his utmost for God's highest, and God validated his ministry. He traveled across Europe and America preaching the gospel, pioneering Christian radio, and publishing in a nascent American market that had just come out of the Civil War. His greatest legacy, however, was the life of surrender he lived that has spurred future generations of laypeople to advance, as Moody had, to full-time ministry.

Your conviction is more important than your condition.

Chapter Thirty-Five

The Golden Generation

*And they that shall be of thee shall build the old waste places: thou
shalt raise up the foundations of many generations; and thou shalt be
called, The repairer of the breach, The restorer of paths to dwell in.*
—Isaiah 58:12

This generation has been called everything but golden. They
have been called a wasted generation, a generation with no
profession of faith, a generation that has been beset with more
deadly diseases than any other.

This generation has seen the advent of HIV/AIDS, multidrug-
resistant tuberculosis, a spiraling teenage pregnancy rate, and cancer
that is expected to overtake coronary artery disease as the number-
one killer in the world by 2015.

This onslaught is because the Devil has seen the potential in this
generation. He "is come down, having great wrath, because he knows
that he hath but a short time" (Revelation 12:12b).

He realizes this generation could bring back the King of Kings and
Lord of Lords, and he wants to do everything to stop that, but he is
a loser. Luke 21:31–32 says, "When ye see these things come to pass,
know ye that the kingdom of God is nigh at hand. Verily I say unto you,
this generation shall not pass away, till all be fulfilled."

A People Who Seek His Face

God has called this generation to give up its shame and wear His glory by seeking His face. He has called this generation to be the golden generation and not a wasted one, but this will happen only if they seek His face.

Psalm 24:6–7 says, "This is the generation of them that seek him, that seek thy face, O Jacob. Lift up your heads, O ye gates and be ye lift up, ye everlasting doors and the King of glory shall come in."

This generation of seekers will seek His face and not His hand, and God has promised them open doors of glory. They will bring back the King in His glory as a glorious generation and not a garbage generation.

Ephesians 5:27 says Jesus "might present it [the church] to himself a glorious church, not having spot, or wrinkle, or any such thing but that it should be holy and without blemish."

While the world has given up hope on this generation, God has not! He promises to "build the old waste places … raise up the foundations of many generations … be [a] repairer of the breach" (Isaiah 58:12).

This generation of glory and restoration starts in the place of prayer and fasting. Isaiah 58:2–3 tells us,

> They seek God daily, and delight to know His ways, as a nation that did righteousness, and forsook not the ordinance of their God. They ask of me the ordinances of justice [and] take delight in approaching to God.

A People Tried in the Fire

One characteristic of our golden generation is that it is tried in the fire. Behind the luster and glow of glory is a fiery trial. In Revelation 8:3, we read, "I counsel thee to buy of me gold tried in the fire, that thou mayest be rich and white raiment, that thou may be clothed, and that the shame of thy nakedness do not appear."

You cannot shine forth as gold unless you are ready to suffer for God. Job 23:10 says, "[God] knows the way that I take: when he hath tried me, I shall come forth as gold." This golden generation will suffer more for Christ than any other. Jesus said,

They [shall] deliver you up to be afflicted, and shall kill you and ye shall be hated of all nations for my name's sake. And then shall many be offended, and shall betray one another, and shall hate one another ... And because iniquity shall abound, the love of many shall wax cold. (Matthew 24:9–12)

As we enter the last days, glory will exponentially increase with our fiery trails and persecutions. In Ephesians 3:13, Paul said, "I desire that ye faint not at my tribulations for you, which is your glory." Our gory situations make for his glorious manifestations in us.

As 1 Peter 4:14 says, "If ye be reproached for the name of Christ, happy are ye; for the spirit of glory and of God resteth upon you: on their part he is evil spoken of, but on your part he is glorified."

We are that golden generation, and nothing the Devil throws against us will deter us from manifesting the love of God and becoming lovers of God. Proverbs 19:11 says, " the discretion of a man defers his anger and it is his glory to pass over a transgression."

My Heavenly Vision

I was on an extended fast seeking God for my nation in 1993. The nation was at a crossroads; the freest and fairest election ever conducted had just been annulled by the dictator General Ibrahim Babangida. I was a third-year medical student at the time and had dedicated my summer holidays to seeking God for my nation by embarking on a twenty-eight-day, water-only fast.

During this time, I experienced God's visitation. I saw a cloud literally descend into my ten-by-twelve-foot room, and an unspeakable glory enveloped it. I was awake but unable to relate with anything or anyone physically. I was in God's presence.

During those few minutes, God spoke words that shaped my life and ministry. He called me to be a "general to this generation" and expounded Psalm 71:18 to me. He assured me that my ministry would affect the world and showed me preaching to millions of people with signs and wonders following.

Out of that vision, Faith and Power Ministries was birthed. A global platform for medical missions and humanitarian services, called

Saints Specialist Services, was also birthed out of that vision, and since then, ministry events, including monthly Holy Ghost Nights and semiannual missions have taken place.

The richest place in the world is not the cemetery, with its untapped potentials, but the Spirit of a man with a living soul.

Chapter Thirty-Six

Total Treasures

We have this treasure in earthen vessels, that the Excellency
of the power may be of God, and not of us.
—2 Corinthians 4:7

We all have treasures in us. Our lives are not accidents; our conceptions were not mistakes. The Creator deliberately formed us and gave us gifts and talents with which to bless the world.

When God brought the children of Israel out of Egypt, He called them a special treasure. In Exodus 19:5, He said, "If ye will obey my voice indeed, and keep my covenant, then ye shall be a peculiar treasure unto me above all people for all the earth is mine."

God did not make you to be just a beneficiary but a benefactor of divine blessings to those who need them. You are a treasure-house and, as the seed of Abraham (according to Galatians 3:16), we must be "the seed [by which] all the nations of the earth [shall] be blessed" (Genesis 22:18).

He said in 1 Peter 2:9, "Ye are a chosen generation, a royal priesthood, an holy nation, a peculiar people; that ye should shew forth the praises of him who hath called you out of darkness into his marvelous light."

Treasures, Not Trash

God does not make trash—only treasures. We are the epitome of glory, power, and honor because we "are created in His image and after His likeness" (Genesis 1:26).

Too many Christians die feeling unappreciated, unwanted, and undervalued even though God has made them treasure-houses. They have failed to discover their treasure within and so live as trash instead of treasure. Just like the children of Israel at Kadesh Barnea, many believers see themselves in their "own sight as grass hoppers and are so in their sight" (Numbers 13:33).

In contrast, God calls them "the apple of his eye" (Zechariah 2:8) who are "graven upon the palms of His hands [and whose] walls are continually before Him" (Isaiah 49:16). You are special to God, not suspicious to Him. Deuteronomy 7:6 says, "You art an holy people unto the Lord thy God: the Lord thy God hath chosen you to be a special people unto himself, above all people that are upon the face of the earth."

In Psalm 8:4–5, the hosts of heaven asked God, "What is man, that thou art mindful of him and the son of man, that thou visits him? For thou hast made him a little lower than the angels, and hast crowned him with glory and honor." The word for *angels* in Psalm 8:5 is *elohim*, meaning "God," but it should be "a little lower than God," which is why Psalm 8:6 says God "has made him [man] to have dominion over the works of thy hands [and] put all things under his feet."

Discover, Not Determine, Your Treasure

In Matthew 13:44, Jesus taught us about discovering what is buried in our lives and valuing it. He said, "The kingdom of heaven is like unto treasure hid in a field ... which when a man hath found, he hides, and for joy thereof goes and sells all that he hath, and buys that field." The man in the parable sold everything he had to obtain this treasure buried in the fields of life. Until we go digging for the treasure, we cannot be a treasure to our generation.

Proverbs 21:20 says, "There is treasure to be desired and oil in the dwelling of the wise but a foolish man spendeth it up." Your desire is the pivot to your discovering and doing God's will, but way too many Christians stay in the describe mode instead of the desire mode.

Go from describing to desiring great things from God and you will discover the treasure within you. The treasure in you will not be manifested when the discoveries for your life are still unknown. Discovery is the key to recovering total treasures in your life.

Jonathan Edwards: The Priceless Power of Discovery

Jonathan Edwards (1703–1758) is considered one of America's greatest preachers. A graduate of Yale University and a one-time president of Princeton, he preached alongside George Whitfield in the first Great Awakening that saw thousands of lives come to Christ in the middle and northeastern parts of the United States.

He preached a fiery sermon, "Sinners in the hands of angry God," in 1737 that spurred widespread repentance and restitution in the area. His church, the Church of Christ in Northampton, Massachusetts, saw more than three hundred people saved in a few months as a result of the revival.

Out of his heritage came a vice president (Aaron Burr), three senators, three governors, three mayors, thirteen presidents of colleges, thirty justices, hundreds of lawyers, sixty-five professors, and hundreds of preachers, businessmen, philanthropists, journalists, and sportsmen. Only one member of this family ever went to jail for a felony.

A New York State government inquisition in the early twentieth century revealed that the family of this famed preacher cost the state of New York less than $5,000 in two hundred years of living in the state. He discovered his purpose for life and did it without compromise.

He was chastised, vilified, and castigated by opponents of grace by faith, who detested the emotionalism exhibited by some at his meetings, but through it all, he labored on till the end. His legacy lives on today in the multiplied generations of missionaries and theologians who have been inspired by his seminal works on freedom of the will, religious affections, and the life and ministry of William Brainerd, missionary to the Indians.

Until there's contention, there can be no contentment.

Chapter Thirty-Seven

The Generation of Glory

How shall not the ministration of the spirit be rather glorious
for if the ministration of condemnation be glory, much more
doth the ministration of righteousness exceed in glory?
—2 Corinthians 3:8–9

This generation, more than any before it, has been called to live gloriously. The glory of Moses in the Old Testament was so great that "the children of Israel could not stedfastly behold his face ... for the glory of his countenance" (2 Corinthians 3:7). In today's new dispensation of salvation through Christ, however,

> even that which was made glorious (in Moses day) had no glory in this respect, by reason of the glory that excelleth for if that which is done away was glorious, much more that which remaineth is glorious. (2 Corinthians 3:10–11)

We are the generation of glory because we have the ministration of the Holy Spirit by righteousness in Christ (2 Corinthians 3:8–9). Unfortunately, glory is celebrated as an exception today while shame is accepted as the rule. That is an anathema!

In Hebrews 2:10, we read, "It became him, for whom are all things, and by whom are all things, in bringing many sons unto glory, to make the captain of their salvation perfect through sufferings."

Glory is not a function of pedigree or position but of destiny. Jesus prayed in John 17:22 that "the glory which thou gave me I have given them [the church] that they may be one, even as we are one." Glory should be our dwelling place, not an occasional hangout.

When God made you, he gave you glory (Psalm 8:5), but the Devil came to steal it and replace it with shame. In 2 Thessalonians 2:14, Paul said God "called you by our gospel, to the obtaining of the glory of our Lord Jesus Christ" and in "a glorious high throne from the beginning is the place of our sanctuary" (Jeremiah 17:12).

Called, Chosen, and Glorified

In Romans 8:30, we read, "Whom [God] did predestinate, them he also called and whom he called, them he also justified and whom he justified, them he also glorified."

Our destiny is to be glorified, not to be shamed. This generation has been deceived by the falsehood of Satan into believing that sin, sorrow, sickness and shame is all it is good for, but the Devil is a liar.

God called and chose you from the foundation of the earth to be glorified. Anything else is counterfeit Christianity. God is not glorified by your shame or despairing but by your celebration and lifting in the spheres of life. You are not a commodity of vanity but a creature of value. Isaiah 60:1–3 says,

> Arise [and] shine for thy light is come and the glory of the Lord is risen upon thee. For, behold, darkness shall cover the earth, and gross darkness the people but the Lord shall arise upon thee, and his glory shall be seen upon thee and Gentiles shall come to thy light, and kings to the brightness of thy rising.

Everyone God made is destined for glory. Satan corrupted the glory in the garden of Eden, but Jesus came to restore it. In Isaiah 61:1, 6–7, the prophet Isaiah prophesied that "the Spirit of the Lord God upon Jesus ... [will cause us to] eat the riches of the Gentiles, and in their glory boast ... [so that] for our shame we shall have double."

In Colossians 1:27, we read, "Christ in you [is] the hope of [our] glory," and in Luke 2:32, Jesus is described as "a light to lighten the

Gentiles, and the glory of thy people Israel." His intention for believers is "to make them inherit the throne of glory" (1 Samuel 2:8) and for "the LORD of hosts [to] be [their] crown of glory and diadem of beauty" (Isaiah 28:5).

Restoring and Recovering Our Destiny of Glory

As 1 Peter 5:1 describes it, Peter was "an elder, and a witness of the sufferings of Christ, and also a partaker of the glory that shall be revealed." The aftermath of betraying Jesus thrice (Matthew 26:69–75) and abandoning his ministry to go fishing was supposed to be shame, but Peter recovered and restored his God-appointed glorious destiny; he said in 1 Peter 1:5 that he was a partaker of the glory of God.

He did not wallow in shame and self-pity but arose as a pillar of the early church and spoke to thousands and performed miracles (Acts 2:14, 3:8, 4:16).

The secret to his restoration and the restoration of a shamed generation is encountering Jesus again. Peter met Jesus on the shore after his shamed setbacks, and Jesus asked him, "Lovest thou me more than these?" (John 21:15).

Peter replied in the affirmative, and Jesus asked him to feed his sheep thrice (John 21:15–17). He told Jesus at the last behest that He "knowest all things" (John 21:17) and he was restored and revived and became a partaker of the glory that shall be revealed.

A generation selflessly in love with God is a generation of glory. Jesus died a shameful death on the cross to change our shame to glory. His blood was shed to recover shameful destinies and make them glorious, but first we must make him Lord of all.

Until Peter saw Jesus as knowing all things, he could not fully actualize his destiny. Proverbs 25:28 says, "He that hath no rule over his own spirit is like a city that is broken down, and without walls." Give God all of you, and He will restore the glory to your life.

The Story of William Colgate

William Colgate (1783–1857) fled religious persecution in England to achieve his God-given dream in New York City. He started the Colgate toothpaste and soap factory after losing his first two businesses.

On his way to New York from Connecticut for his third business endeavor, he met a Christian canal boat captain who told him, "Give yours heart to Christ; give God all that belongs to Him and make an honest soap. If someone is to be the leading soap maker in New York, it may as well be you."

Colgate began giving God 10 percent of his profits and later increased it to 90 percent as his business grew. He gave to different gospel causes such as the American Bible Society and Hamilton Theological Center (now called Colgate University) and supported building projects of the Baptist Convention.

He was acknowledged by the missions board of his church as the sole sponsor of several missionaries. His company, Colgate Palmolive, is today worth over $17 billion and has penetrated over two hundred countries with its products.

His prosperity started as a donor. He honored God with his giving and ended extremely fruitful because of the God who has power to give wealth. Deuteronomy 8:18 says, "But thou shalt remember the LORD thy God: for it is he that giveth thee power to get wealth, that he may establish his covenant which he sware unto thy fathers, as it is this day."

Feigning is the reason for fallow living.

Chapter Thirty-Eight

Guaranteed Glory

But as truly as I live, all the earth shall be filled with the glory of the LORD.
—Numbers 14:21

God's glory is guaranteed. According to Numbers 14:21, it will certainly cover the earth whether we believe it or not. It is not a conditional promise but a certain promise that is predicated on the eternal life of God.

If God is alive, glory must be evident on the earth, and the only cause for glory to disappear would be for God to die, which is impossible. The church needs to elevate its expectation for glory and see it as a lifestyle, not an exceptional matter.

What you don't anticipate, you won't participate in because as a "man thinks in his heart so is he" (Proverbs 23:7). The glorious life must become an accepted norm for every Christian and the earth-covering glory a benchmark of what we should expect.

Habakkuk 2:14 says, "The earth shall be filled with the knowledge of the glory of the LORD, as the waters cover the sea." Get ready for the glory.

The Shame Sham

The shame sham in the church is a satanically orchestrated deceit. It has no basis in Scripture and is more a creation of minds and emotions than of the Word and will of God. The picture of victims living in defeat and despondency is not the image of the church triumphant Jesus died for.

The lack of wisdom about what God says about us, the church, is the principal reason for the shame sham bedeviling the church today. Until we discover our glorious destinies, we will not recover from the shame the world and the Devil have put upon us.

The blood of Jesus is the solution to sin; you need no other elixir. He died, rose, and is seated at the right hand of God today to ensure that you walk, live, and manifest His glory.

The reason for lack of glory is insufficient knowledge of what God's Word says about it. Until we understand His manifold grace, we cannot manifest glory to the world. As 1 Peter 4:10–11 says,

> As good stewards of the manifold grace of God ... let us speak as the oracles of God [and] if any man minister, let him do it as of the ability which God giveth that God in all things may be glorified through Jesus Christ.

Shamelessness: Signed, Sealed, and Settled

In 2 Peter 1:3–4, God "called us to glory and virtue [and] gave us exceeding great and precious promises that by these we might be partakers of His divine nature." Before you were born, glory was already your status quo.

The church is described as a replica of God on earth in 1 John 4:17: "As He is, so are we in this world." The psalmist called us gods, not mere men (Psalm 82:6), which Jesus corroborated in John 10:35: "[The psalmist] called them gods, unto whom the word of God came, and the scripture cannot be broken."

God made us replicas of His glory, and we were not to be ashamed. That is why Adam and Eve "were both naked, the man and his wife, and not ashamed" (Genesis 2:25). Glory is our heritage, and we must dwell in it because it is a God-given guarantee.

Isaiah 43:7 says, "Every one that is called by my name ... I have created him for my glory; I have formed him; yea, I have made him." You were not made for shame but for glory. It is not attained by some achievement but given at birth. The fullness of His glory is, however, manifested only after faith in Jesus Christ and by walking in the Spirit.

From Schizophrenic to Supernatural

Gary Whetstone is the senior pastor of Victory Christian Fellowship in Delaware. A multitalented and gifted pastor and preacher, Gary and his wife, Faye, have been pastors for over thirty-five years and have seen God expand their ministry worldwide.

He is the president of Gary Whetstone Worldwide Ministries and has developed an online Bible curriculum with video and audio productions that have enabled laypeople in rural areas to obtain degrees in ministry.

He holds a doctorate in religious education and has impacted hundreds of thousands of lives with his teachings. It did not, however, start this way. Gary went from being labeled a schizophrenic to what he is today.

In his teenage years, Gary became entangled with drugs, sex, violence, a motorcycle gang, and a destructive lifestyle following a car accident. He became so violent and suicidal that he entered a mental health institution.

He was scheduled to undergo an electronic lobotomy of the brain and, as a result, be confined for life with the brain of a three-year-old. One day, however, he heard a voice telling him to run, and he started to run. He ran out of the hospital in a borrowed coat and shoes and was hit by a car driven by one of the hospital's clinical psychologists.

Instead of immediately calling the police, as she would otherwise have done, she pulled to the side of the road. God told her, "Do not call the police because he is mine." She told Dr. Whetstone this fifteen years later, when she heard his testimony on radio.

While he was waiting for a fake ID and preparing for life as a fugitive in the marshes of Florida, God directed him to drive back to the mental institution and ask the hospital to let him undergo every possible test. He obeyed God and returned to Delaware, and the results confirmed God's supernatural healing.

The findings confirmed Gary's assertion that he was sane, and they said he had no clinical reason for ever being termed insane.

They originally planned to lobotomize him for a brain tumor, but that was canceled, and Gary was discharged without any follow-up or medications.

Whetstone left the hospital that day and has been preaching the life-giving gospel of Jesus Christ ever since. He has been married for almost forty years, has two children and six grandchildren, and has seen countless miracles when he prayed for the sick and infirmed. His life is a testimony of a healing life that went from schizophrenic to supernatural.

PART VIII

Conclusion

His gentleness makes for your glory but your stubbornness makes for your shame.

Chapter Thirty-Nine

Epilogue

The blessing of the Lord, *it maketh rich, and he addeth no sorrow [or shame] with it.*
—Proverbs 10:22

S hame is the church's worst enemy. It is self-afflicted but can be gotten rid of by the blood of Jesus and appropriating the benefits of the cross of Calvary in our lives today.

Shame cripples prayer and sabotages praise. It makes the altar a meaningless tool for kingdom domination because there is no confidence or assurance at the altar. It removes passion for the lost and denigrates one's value in the eyes of God.

This does not have to be the case. Jesus came to restore the glory in the church and abrogate shame permanently from its midst. He destroyed it at the cross and permanently revoked its ownership of our temples by shedding His blood at Golgotha.

Mephibosheth: The Shame Destroyer

Mephibosheth means "shame destroyer" in Hebrew. This son of Jonathan, born during David's covenant relationship with Jonathan, was named Mephibosheth because covenant always destroys shame.

As long as the covenant between Jonathan and David was in effect (1 Samuel 18:3), Mephibosheth knew he would one day move out of shame and into glory. His situation at the time was, however, personified by shame.

He was crippled from age five (2 Samuel 4:4), orphaned by the deaths of his father and grandfather, ostracized by the ruling class because of his heritage, living in Lodebar (meaning "land of no pasture"), and had no assets.

One day, though, the reality of his name manifested. In 2 Samuel 9:1, David asked, "Is there yet any that is left of the house of Saul, that I may shew him kindness for Jonathan's sake?" David immediately moved Mephibosheth from Lodebar to the king's palace and made the palace accountable for all and his family's provisions forthwith.

Jesus shed his blood in covenant for us as David and Jonathan did for Mephibosheth. Hebrews 12:24 says, "Jesus [is] the mediator of the new covenant, and of the blood of sprinkling, that speaketh better things than that of Abel."

Jesus' covenant blood on the mercy seat destroys shame and grants us divine glory. The seemingly impossible situations Mephibosheth faced were swallowed up by the invisible power of covenant.

Your shame is destroyed because the Son of God gave His life to give you the covenant promise of glory (Isaiah 61:7). God said in Psalm 89:34, "My covenant will I not break, nor alter the thing that is gone out of my lips."

Contacts

Faith and Power Ministries is dedicated to showing the power of God once again to this generation. It is dedicated to ushering in the last-days' glory of God and, in the course of doing so, turning lives around for the kingdom of God.

Our email is tobemomah@yahoo.com, and we can be contacted via email or via our website, www.faithandpowerministries.org. We reside in West Monroe, Louisiana, and can be reached at PO Box 550, West Monroe, Louisiana, 71294, USA.

Other Books by Tobe Momah

A General and a Gentleman (biography of General Sam Momah) Spectrum Books, 2003.

Between the Systems, Soul, and Spirit of Man (a Christian doctor's view on sickness and its source) Xulon Press, 2007.

Building Lasting Relationships (a manual for the complete home) Xulon Press, 2006.

Metrobiology: A Study of Life in the City, First Edition (a doctor's daily devotional) Xulon Press, 2008.

Pregnancy: Pitfalls, Pearls and Principles, Westbow Press, 2011.

Ultimate Harvest: Five F.A.C.T.S. on Fruitfulness and How to Grow the American Church Again, Westbow Press, 2012.

From Edginess to Eagerness: Taking the Church Back to Willing Service, Westbow Press, 2012.

Fear no Evil ... By Hating Evil, Westbow Press, 2013.

Fear no Evil ... By Hating Evil (a daily devotional) Westbow Press, 2013.

Healing Lives (true stories of encouragement and achievement in the midst of sickness) Westbow Press, 2014.